THE MIDI RESOURCE BOOK

by STEVE DE FURIA &
JOE SCACCIAFERRO

Produced by John Cerullo
Art Direction by John Flannery
Cover Photo by George Mauro
Additional Technical Editing by Jon Eiche

Produced and Published by
Third Earth Publishing Inc.
Pompton Lakes, N.J.

Distributed Exclusively by Hal Leonard Books.

ISBN 0 - 88188 587 - 8

Acknowledgement

Collection of the data for these books was an enormous task. We would like to thank the MIDI Manufacturers Association, the Japanese MIDI Standards Committee, and the International MIDI Association, as well as the engineers and designers from the many manufacturers who contributed to this effort. In particular we would like to thank Jim Cooper, Chris Meyer, Jim Mothersbaugh, Paul M. Young, Jerry Kovarsky, Dan Ramsauer, Mark Koenig, Alex Limberis and the staff at Triple S Electronics for their assistance and support.

Introduction

Less than five years ago, every brand of synthesizer had its own, non-compatible type of interface (if it had any interface at all!). Not only did this make it impossible to attach one to another, it discouraged third-party developers from getting started. MIDI changed all of this.

It may be too early to evaluate the impact of MIDI on the world of music: we are still riding the crest of what has been called "the wave of the future." Musicians working in Jazz, Pop, Rock, and even Classical disciplines have had their possibilities virtually explode around them. But explosions can have positive or negative results, and many of these musicians are not sure whether they should jump aboard or duck the shrapnel.

The problem for most musicians is threefold:

Firstly, despite the fact that MIDI is electrically just supposed to be a plug and a jack as far as the user is concerned, MIDI is a very participatory interface: rarely is the musician satisfied to just have two pieces of equipment attached. His system grows to three, four, dozens of pieces. This requires a "systems engineering" type of approach that can be confusing to the newcomer.

Secondly, MIDI has a rich set of possibilites. There are many possible commands, several modes of operation, and a hundred different System Exclusive messages that may or may not be of concern.

Finally, there are a plethora of accessory boxes available to aid and confuse the issue. Switch boxes, Mappers, and Mergers have all become an important adjunct to sequencers, drum machines, and synthesizers. But few really know how to use them (or even that they need them). So what is a poor musician to do? Get MIDI educated!

It is important that the end-user musician (or the interested engineer or programmer) gain as much basic understanding of the underlying concepts of MIDI as he can. If he can grasp the real basics of the MIDI specifications, it is a short step to understanding how we can apply the various MIDI tools to his needs.

The MIDI Resource Book is designed to be a guide through the MIDI maze. In conjunction with the other two books in the series, **The MIDI Implementation Book** and **The MIDI System Exclusive Book**, it can act as both a dictionary and an encyclopedia on the subject of MIDI. It explains the MIDI 1.0 Specification, which is the root of MIDI. It also covers the very newest extensions of MIDI, including the Sample Dump Standard and the MIDI Time Code. Also included is a directory of manufacturers, organizations, bulletin boards, and publications that deal with MIDI.

One thing that has become clear in the last couple of years is that MIDI is not going to stand still. In that time, the Sample Dump Standard, MIDI Time Code, and the Registered/Non-Registered Controller concept have all come into use. Approximately a dozen controller I.D.s have also been defined in this time. The Ferro Technology MIDI Reference Books will not stand still either. Their update service will make sure that your information doesn't lag behind the MIDI scene.

Jim Cooper
President MMA

1. Guide To The MIDI Reference Series

In This Section....6
About The Conventions Used In This Book....7
How To Use The MIDI Reference Books....8
About The Double Listing System....10

2. Inside MIDI

In This Section....12
MIDI At A Glance....13
- Overview....14
- Detailed Summaries....17

Sample Dump Standard Operation and Communication Details....25
- Flowchart....26
- Communication Protocols....27

Applying MIDI Information....30
- Application Notes For New Designers....31
- Converting Hex / Binary / Decimal MIDI Data Values....32
- Notes For Using System Exclusive Data....36
- Using Implementation Charts....37
  - Applications....37
  - Reading Implementation Charts....38
    - General Comments....38
    - Chart Summary....39
  - Filling Out MIDI Implementation Charts....44
    - General Comments....44
    - Chart Summary....44

3. Specification Details

In This Section 48
MIDI 1.0 Specification 49
Outline 50
The Specification 51
MIDI 1.0 Specification Updates 63
Manufacturer ID Codes 64
MIDI Controller Definitions 66
Using Registered and Non-Registered Parameters 69
System Exclusive Extensions 70
Sample Dump Standard 72
Overview 73
The Standard 75
MIDI Time Code Specification 78
Overview 79
Detailed Specification 82
Manufacturer's System Exclusive Formats 93
Introduction 94
Akai 95
Casio 103
Kawai 105
Korg 107
Roland 109
Yamaha 120
Terminology Guide 130

4. References and Resources

In This Section 134
MIDI Organizations 135
Manufacturers 137
On-Line Resources / Electronic Bulletin Boards 140
Education Sources 142
Books and Publications 144
Technical Support Facilities 146
Registration Form 148

SECTION 1: GUIDE TO THE MIDI REFERENCE SERIES

In this section:

About The Conventions Used In This Book

How To Use The MIDI Reference Books

A "road map" to the three books in the series describing how to use them together as one master reference.

About The Double-Listing System

Instructions on how to use the Application and Product Listings used to organize implementation charts and System Exclusive listings in **The MIDI Implementation Book** and **The MIDI System Exclusive Book**.

About The Conventions Used In This Book

There is no standardized way of presenting MIDI message content and format details. In the *Specification Updates, Sample Dump Standard*, and *MIDI At A Glance* sections of this book we have included message summaries for all defined MIDI messages. The following conventions are used in our message content and format summaries.

EXAMPLE:

<CONTROL CHANGE> (Status byte)
    <Control Number> (Data byte)
    <Control Value> (Data byte)
Bn cc vv
n= channel number 0-F
cc = controller number 00-79
vv = controller value 00-7F

OR

<CONTROL CHANGE> <Control Number> <Control Value>
    Bn cc vv
n= channel number 0-F
cc = controller number 00-79
vv = controller value 00-7F

- Message, status, and data names are given in **Boldface type.**
- Byte-specific information is enclosed in angle brackets "< >".
- When space permits, message bytes are listed vertically with data bytes indented from status bytes. Otherwise, they are listed horizontally.
- Comments are enclosed in parenthesis.

The hex message summaries also include the hexadecimal form of the message as well.

- Hex constants are given as UPPER CASE letters.
- Variables are given in lower-case letters.
- The range of variable values is given in hex.

How To Use The MIDI Reference Books

Within the Ferro Music Technology Series™, **The MIDI Resource Book**, **The MIDI Implementation Book**, and **The MIDI System Exclusive Book** form a series within a series. If you are involved with MIDI as an engineer or computer programmer, then you are undoubtedly already familiar with reference and resource books. You'll find that these three books form a long overdue, and invaluable, desk reference set.

If your involvement with MIDI is based on a more practical user's point of view, then the concept (and usefulness) of such a reference work might be new to you. So we thought a few words on what these books are, and how to get the most from them, might be helpful here.

The tools and techniques we use to create, produce, and perform music incorporate increasingly more MIDI concepts into both their design and operation. Therefore, the musician who can understand and exploit MIDI concepts can take best advantage of the tools made available via this technology. The MIDI Reference Series is designed to help you to both understand MIDI technology and put that understanding to practical use.

The MIDI Resource Book is your source of information about MIDI concepts, standard conventions, and specifications. Use this book to learn what MIDI means and how it works. When you understand the information in this book you'll know how MIDI concepts can be applied to any application, and you will be able to get the most from the data in the other two books.

Use **The MIDI Implementation Book** and **The MIDI System Exclusive Book** to learn the practical details of how MIDI has been utilized in a particular device, and how it can be used effectively with other units in a MIDI system. You'll find that these books can be invaluable if you want to know how well one MIDI instrument can control (or be controlled by) another, or when you're looking for a device to solve a particular interfacing problem. If you're shopping for a new addition to your MIDI system, you'll find that comparing implementations and system exclusive functions of similar instruments can help you make an informed choice as to which instrument best fits your needs.

Of course, as MIDI and related products evolve, Ferro Technologies will release updated versions of these books.

The MIDI Resource Book

This book is the core to our "series within a series." It contains up-to-date MIDI specifications and standards documentation. In it you'll find MMA and JMSC documentation for:

The Complete MIDI 1.0 Specification
The MIDI Sample Dump Standard
Manufacturer's Published System Exclusive Formats

We have provided supplemental sections to each of the above documents that contain further explanations, reference charts, and more. For example, the sections on How to Read and Use MIDI Implementation Charts and Interpreting System Exclusive Codes will give you the keys to unlocking any instrument's full MIDI potential.

This is a true engineering reference. All of the information is logically organized and cross-referenced to provide quick and easy access to any MIDI specification-related details.

The MIDI Resource Book also contains a complete directory of MIDI related references and resources. In it, you'll find listings of:

MIDI Manufacturers
MIDI Organizations
Electronic Bulletin Boards
Related Books and Publications

The MIDI Implementation Book
In this book, there are over 200 complete Implementation Charts from over 30 makers of MIDI devices. These charts (collected with assistance of the MMA, JMSC, IMA, and many independent MIDI manufacturers) represent virtually every type of MIDI product on the market today.

We've provided a unique *double-listing system* that allows you to locate any Implementation Chart within the book by two different methods. Use the **Product Listing** when you want to locate a specific product, and the **Application Listing** when you are looking for a device that meets particular MIDI criteria, or if you want to compare MIDI implementations of similar devices.

The ✣ symbol is our cross-reference symbol. When you see it in entries in either Listing, it indicates that System Exclusive data and/or detailed programming data for that device can be found in **The MIDI System Exclusive Book.**

The MIDI System Exclusive Book
System Exclusive codes are used to perform instrument specific functions and operations that don't fall under the realm of Voice, Mode, Common, and Real Time MIDI messages defined by the MIDI specification. This book contains the complete listing of all system exclusive codes registered with the MMA. It also contains any additional programming information, such as parameter tables and bit-maps, made available by the manufacturers for a given product (or products).

The data in this book is organized with the same *double-listing system* used in **The MIDI Implementation Book.** You can locate information by manufacturer/product with **Product Listing**, or use the **Application Listing** to locate devices by functional description.

The ✣ symbol indicates that an Implementation Chart for that device can be found in **The MIDI Implementation Book.**

About The Double-Listing System

The double-listing system used in **The MIDI Implementation Book** and **The MIDI System Exclusive Book** allows you to locate information by two methods. The **Product Listing** lets you find data quickly when you need information for a specific product. The **Application Listing** allows you to locate data for devices designed for specific applications.

Product Listing
The **Product Listing** is an alphabetized list of manufacturers. Each manufacturer's products are, in-turn, listed in alphabetical order. To find a specific device, find the manufacturer and then locate the device you're looking for in the product list.

Each item in the list shows the *Model, Version,* and *Description* fields as they appear in the actual implementation chart, and the page number where the data can be found. Many of the items will also have this symbol ✣ . It indicates that data for the product is contained in both **The MIDI Implementation Book** and **The MIDI System Exclusive Book**. You can tell at a glance if additional data is available without having to flip through a second book.

Application Listing
The **Application Listing** organizes the products into twenty-two general applications as follows:

Digital Synthesizers	**Interfaces**
Hybrid Synthesizers	**MIDI Data Routing Units**
Samplers	**Synchronization Devices**
Pianos	**MIDI Control Devices**
Preset Instruments	**Channel Converters**
Organs	**CV Converters**
Accordians	**Lighting Controllers**
Performance Controllers	**Data Storage**
Sequencers	**Data Display**
Drum Machines	**Software**
Audio Processors	**Modifications**

Where appropriate, the products listed within each application are further categorized according to *TYPE* , *ON-BOARD CONTROLLER,* or *COMPUTER /INTERFACE*

> *TYPE* is used to further qualify products within a particular application. For example, **Audio Processors** is subdivided into the following types of devices: *Effects, Reverbs, Mixers, Mutes,* and *Volume Controls.*
>
> *ON-BOARD CONTROLLER* is used to indicate the type of controller built-in to performance instruments. You can see which instruments use *Guitar, Percussion,* or *Keyboard* controllers to generate MIDI Note On/Off messages. Instruments that can only be controlled remotely by another device are indicated with the word *Slave.* In addition, instruments with built-in sequencers are indicated with the word *Sequencer.*
>
> *COMPUTER/INTERFACE* lists the type of computer and/or interface required by software products.

Within the categories *TYPE, ON-BOARD CONTROLLER,* and *COMPUTER/INTERFACE,* they are listed alphabetically by manufacturer. Each item in the **Application Listing** shows the *Manufacturer, Model,* and *Version* fields as they appear on the Implementation Chart and appropriate *TYPE, ON-BOARD CONTROLLER,* or *COMPUTER/INTERFACE* notes. The ✣ symbol is used to indicate that data for an item is contained in both books. The page number shows where the data can be found in this book.

SECTION 2: INSIDE MIDI

In this section:

MIDI At A Glance

Of particular interest to engineers, programmers, and others who need an accurate, easy-to-use reference that integrates all hardware and software details of the updated MIDI 1.0 specification.

- Overview

  A logically organized, concise presentation highlighting all aspects of the MIDI spec and updates.

- Detailed Summaries

  Detailed descriptions of data and message formats, transmit/receive summaries of the four MIDI Modes, and hex summaries with descriptions of all defined MIDI messages.

Sample Dump Standard Operation and Communication Details

- Flowchart

  Diagram detailing Sample Dump operation flow.

- Communication Protocols

  Diagrams detailing use of the data request and handshaking messages as defined in the Sample Dump Standard.

Applying MIDI Information

- Application Notes For New Designers

  How to use implementation, System Exclusive, and communication protocol information as design aids.

- Converting Hex/Binary/Decimal MIDI Data Values

  MIDI information is often given in decimal, hex, and binary formats. These tables will help you convert numbers from one numbering system to another.
  - Using The Conversion Tables
  - Table 1: 4-Bit Binary/Hex/Decimal
  - Table 2: 8-Bit Hex/Decimal

- Notes For Using System Exclusive Data
  - Some application ideas for System Exclusive messages.

- Using Implementation Charts
  - General Applications:

    How to use implementation charts as problem-solving tools.
  - Reading Implementation Charts:

    Including notes detailing commonly found "inconsistencies" as well as item-by-item descriptions, details, and points to look for covering each of the entries on a standard implementation chart.
  - Filling Out MIDI Implementation Charts: Guidelines for makers of MIDI devices detailing how to fill out an implementation chart properly and effectively (conforms with MMA instructions), including general conventions to use and item-by-item instructions for each entry on the chart.

1.0 HARDWARE

1.1 Transmission
- 31.25 kBaud
- Asynchronous
- Start bit/8 data bits/Stop bit

1.2 Circuit
- 5 mA current loop
- Logic 0 is current ON
- One output shall drive one input only
- Input opto-isolated
- Input requires less than 5 mA to turn on

1.3 Connectors
- DIN 5-pin, female, panel mount
- Pins 1 & 3 not used and left unconnected
- Labelled "MIDI IN" and "MIDI OUT"

1.4 Cables
- Maximum length: 50 feet
- Ends terminate with DIN 5-pin, male
- Shielded, twisted pair

1.5 MIDI THRU
- Optional
- Direct copy of MIDI IN data
- Labelled "MIDI THRU"

2.0 DATA FORMATS

2.1 Byte Formats
- Status Bytes: Most Significant Bit is set (binary 1)
- Data Bytes: Most Significant Bit is reset (binary 0)

2.2 Message Formats
- Channel Voice, Channel Mode, and System Common formats: Status byte followed by 0 or more data bytes
- System Real Time format: single status byte
- System Exclusive formats:
  - Must start with SysEx and ID
  - Can contain any number of data bytes
  - Must end with EOX

2.3 Operational Conventions
- Except for Real Time, new Status bytes always command the receiver to adopt their status. Even if new Status byte is received before last message was completed.

2.3.1 Running Status
- For Voice and Mode messages only
- Once Status byte is received and processed, status remains the same until different Status byte is received
- Repeated Status bytes may be omitted (optional)
- Correct number of Data bytes must be sent in correct order
- Receivers must recognize Running Status formats
- Real Time messages interrupt Running Status temporarily
- Any other Status byte stops Running Status

2.3.2 Unimplemented Status
- Status bytes for unimplemented functions should be ignored
- Subsequent Data bytes ignored

2.3.3 Undefined Status Bytes
- Undefined Status bytes may not be used
- If received, they must be ignored
- Subsequent data must be ignored

3.0 CHANNEL MESSAGES
- Intended for any units in system whose channel number matches the channel number encoded in the Status byte

3.1 Channel Voice Messages
3.1.1 **<NOTE OFF>**
<Key Number>
< Note Off Velocity>
3.1.2 **<NOTE ON>**
<Key Number>
<Velocity>
3.1.3 **<POLYPHONIC KEY PRESSURE>**
<Key Number>
<Pressure Value>
3.1.4 **<CONTROL CHANGE>**
<Controller Number>
<Controller Value>
3.1.5 **<PROGRAM CHANGE>**
<Program Number>
3.1.6 **<CHANNEL PRESSURE>**
<Pressure Value>
3.1.7 **<PITCH WHEEL CHANGE>**
<P.Whl.Change LSB>
<P.Whl.Change MSB>

3.2 MIDI Modes
3.2.1 OMNI ON/POLY (Mode 1)
3.2.2 OMNI ON/MONO (Mode 2)
3.2.3 OMNI OFF/POLY (Mode 3)
3.2.4 OMNI OFF/MONO (Mode 4)

3.3 Channel Mode Messages
3.3.1 **LOCAL CONTROL OFF**
3.3.2 **LOCAL CONTROL ON**
3.3.3 **ALL NOTES OFF**
3.3.4 **OMNI MODE OFF (ALL NOTES OFF)**
3.3.5 **OMNI MODE ON (ALL NOTES OFF)**
3.3.6 **MONO MODE ON (ALL NOTES OFF)**
3.3.7 **POLY MODE ON (ALL NOTES OFF)**

4.0 SYSTEM MESSAGES
- Status bytes not encoded with channel numbers

4.1 System Common Messages
- Intended for all units in system

4.1.1 **<QUARTER FRAME>**
<TYPE/DATA>
4.1.2 **<SONG POSITION POINTER>**
< Pointer LSB>
<Pointer MSB>
4.1.3 **<SONG SELECT>**
<Song Number>
4.1.4 **<TUNE REQUEST>**
4.1.5 **<EOX>**

4.2 System Real Time Messages
- Intended for all units in system

4.2.1 **<TIMING CLOCK>**
4.2.2 **<START>**
4.2.3 **<CONTINUE>**
4.2.4 **<STOP>**
4.2.5 **<ACTIVE SENSING>**
4.2.6 **<SYSTEM RESET>**

4.3 System Exclusive Messages
- Intended only for units that recognize specific System Exclusive ID

4.3.1 Manufacturer System Exclusive
- Specified by Manufacturer ID code
- Format:

<SysEx>
<Manufacturer ID>
<data>
<EOX>

4.3.2 Universal Non-Real Time System Exclusive
- Specified by Universal Non-Real Time ID (7EH)

4.3.2.1 **SAMPLE DUMP HEADER**
4.3.2.2 **SAMPLE DUMP DATA PACKET**
4.3.2.3 **DUMP REQUEST**
4.3.2.4 **SET UP**
4.3.2.5 **WAIT**
4.3.2.6 **CANCEL**
4.3.2.7 **NAK**
4.3.2.8 **ACK**

4.3.3 Universal Real Time System Exclusive
- Specified by Universal Real Time ID (7FH)

4.3.3.1 **FULL MESSAGE**
4.3.3.2 **USER BITS**

4.3.4 Universal Non-Commercial System Exclusive
- Specified by Universal Non-Commerical ID (7DH)

1.0 HARDWARE

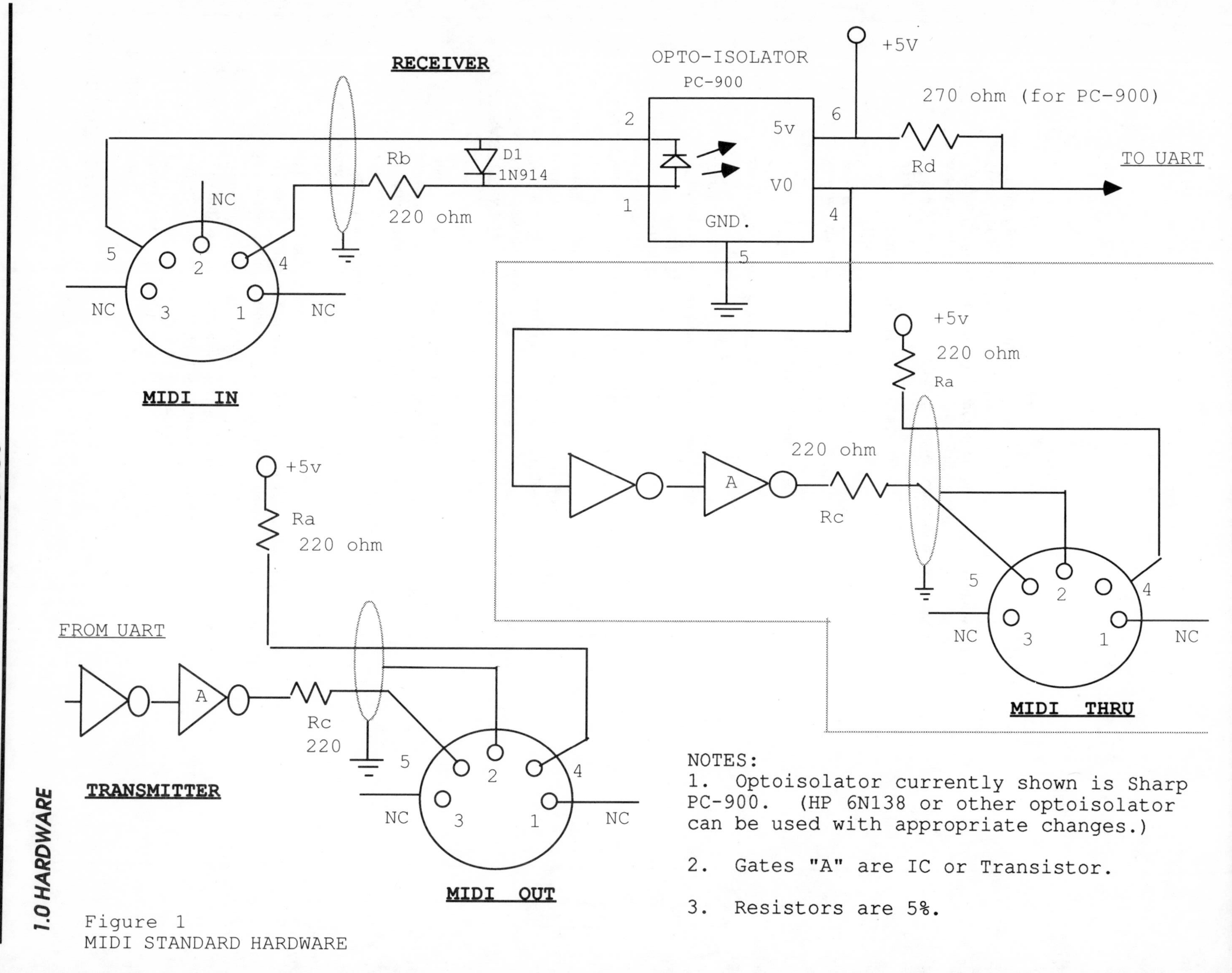

NOTES:
1. Optoisolator currently shown is Sharp PC-900. (HP 6N138 or other optoisolator can be used with appropriate changes.)
2. Gates "A" are IC or Transistor.
3. Resistors are 5%.

Figure 1
MIDI STANDARD HARDWARE

2.0 DATA FORMATS

2.1 BYTE FORMATS

2.1.1 Status Bytes

• Bit 7 is always set **<1 x x x n n n n >**

• The four low-order bits (nnnn) of Channel Message Status bytes are used to identify one of 16 channels. Bits 4, 5, and 6 specify one of seven Channel Message Status types.

• The four high-order bits of System Message Status bytes are always set (binary 1). The four low-order bits specify one of 16 System Status bytes (11 are currently defined).

2.1.2 Data Bytes

• Bit 7 is always reset **<0 x x x x x x x>**

• Since bit 7 must always be reset to 0 in a MIDI Data byte, the maximum range of values conveyed by a single byte is 0-127 (00-7FH). Messages that require a larger range of values, convey the value's MSB and LSB in two or more MIDI Data bytes.

2.2 MESSAGE FORMATS

• Each MIDI message consists of a single Status byte followed by 0 or more data bytes. The basic formats for the different types of messages are outlined here. The specific hex codes for every defined message are given in the *Hex Message Summaries* in sections 3 and 4 below.

2.2.1 Channel Voice, Channel Mode, and System Common Formats

<Status>

<Data 1>

<Data 2>

• The number of Data bytes in the message is defined by the particular Status byte.

2.2.2 System Real Time Format

<Status>

• Each message consists of a single Status byte.

2.2.3 System Exclusive Formats

<SysEx>

<ID>

<Data> (any number of bytes)

<EOX>

• The basic format for all System Exclusive messages is the same. A message must start with the System Exclusive Status byte followed by a System Exclusive ID code. Any number of Data bytes may follow the ID code. The last byte of a System Exclusive message must always be the End Of Exclusive Status byte.

<SysEx>
<ID: Manufacturer>
<Data> (any number of bytes)
<EOX>

• The Manufacturer System Exclusive message consists of the System Exclusive Status byte, Manufacturer ID, and any number of Data bytes followed by the End Of Exclusive Status byte. Details of the formats used must be published by the manufacturer. (See *Specification Updates* for Manufacturer's ID codes and *Manufacturer's System Exclusive Formats* and **The MIDI System Exclusive Book** for published codes.)

<SysEx>
<ID:Universal Non-Real Time> (7EH)
<DeviceChannel>
<Sub-ID1>
<Sub-ID2>
<Data> (any number of bytes)
<EOX>

• In a Universal Non-Real Time System Exclusive message, the Universal Non-Real Time identifier follows the System Exclusive Status byte.

Next is a Device Channel number, used to identify which device(s) in the system the message is intended for. A Device Channel value of 127 (7FH) indicates the message is intended for all devices in the system. The Sub-ID identifies the specific message. Any number of Data Bytes may follow, depending on the particular Sub-ID's. The final byte in the message is the End Of Exclusive Status byte.

<SysEx>
<ID:Universal Real Time> (7FH)
<Device Channel>
<Sub-ID1>
<Sub-ID2>
<Data> (any number of bytes)
<EOX>

• The basic format for Universal Real Time System Exclusive messages is the same as used for Non-Real Time messages. Any number of data bytes may follow the Sub ID's (dependent on the particular message they define). The final byte in the message is the End Of Exclusive Status byte.

<SysEx>
<ID:Universal Non-Commercial> (7DH)
<Data> (any number of bytes)
<EOX>

• The basic format for Universal Non-Commercial System Exclusive messages consists of the System Exclusive Status byte, the Universal Non-Commericial Identifier, and any number of Data bytes. The final byte of the message is the End Of Exclusive Status byte. As of this printing, no specific Universal Non-Commercial messages have been formally defined.

3.0 CHANNEL MESSAGE SUMMARIES

3.1 CHANNEL VOICE MESSAGE HEX SUMMARIES

3.1.1 **<NOTE OFF>**
<Key Number>
<Note Off Velocity>

8n kk vv
n = Channel Number 0-F
kk = Key Number 00-7F
vv = Note Off Velocity 00-7F

3.1.2 **<NOTE ON>**
<Key Number>
<Velocity>

9n kk vv
n = Channel Number 0-F
kk = Key Number 00-7F
vv = Velocity 01-7F [00 = NOTE OFF]

3.1.3 **<POLYPHONIC KEY PRESSURE>**
<Key Number>
<Pressure Value>

An kk vv
n = Channel Number 0-F
kk = Key Number 00-7F
vv = Pressure Value 00-7F

3.1.4 **<CONTROL CHANGE>**
<Control Number>
<Control Value>

Bn cc vv
n = Channel Number 0-F
cc = Control Number 00-79
vv = Control Value 00-7F

3.1.5 **<PROGRAM CHANGE>**
<Program Number>

Cn pp
n = Channel Number 0-F
pp = Program Number 00-7F

3.1.6 **<CHANNEL PRESSURE>**
<Pressure Value>

Dn vv
n = Channel Number 0-F
vv = Pressure Value 00-7F

3.1.7 **<PITCH WHEEL CHANGE>**
<P. Whl. Change LSB>
<P. Whl. Change MSB>

En ll hh
n = Channel Number 0-F
ll = Pitch Wheel Change LSB 00-7F
hh = Pitch Wheel Change MSB 00-7F

3.2 MIDI MODE SUMMARIES

3.2.1 ***OMNI ON/POLY [Mode 1]***

• Receiver: Voice Messages are recognized from all channels and assigned to voices polyphonically.

• Transmitter: Voice Messages for all voices are transmitted on the assigned Basic Channel.

3.2.2 ***OMNI ON/MONO [Mode 2]***

• Receiver: Voice messages are recognized from all channels and assigned to one monophonic voice.

• Transmitter: Voice Messages for a single voice are transmitted on the assigned Basic Channel.

3.2.3 ***OMNI OFF/POLY [Mode 3]***

• Receiver: Voice Messages are recognized from assigned Basic Channel and assigned to all voices polyphonically.

• Transmitter: Voice Messages for all voices are transmitted on the assigned Basic Channel.

3.2.4 ***OMNI OFF/MONO [Mode 4]***

• Receiver: Voice Messages are recognized on the assigned Basic Channel through (Basic Channel + M) -1 and assigned monophonically to voices 1 through M respectively. The number of voices assigned (M) is specified by the value of the second byte of the MONO MODE ON message (see *Mode Message Summaries* below).

• Transmitter: Voice Messages for voices 1 through M are transmitted, one voice per channel, on the assigned Basic Channel through (Basic Channel + M) -1 respectively.

3.3 CHANNEL MODE MESSAGE HEX SUMMARIES

3.3.1 **LOCAL CONTROL OFF**
Bn 7A 00
n = Channel Number 0-F

3.3.2 **LOCAL CONTROL ON**
Bn 7A 7F
n = Channel Number 0-F

3.3.3 **ALL NOTES OFF**
Bn 7B 00
n = Channel Number 0-F

3.3.4 **OMNI MODE OFF (ALL NOTES OFF)**
Bn 7C 00
n = Channel Number 0-F

3.3.5 **OMNI MODE ON (ALL NOTES OFF)**
Bn 7D 00
n = Channel Number 0-F

3.3.6 **MONO MODE ON (ALL NOTES OFF)**
Bn 7E mm
n = Channel Number 0-F
mm = number of MONO Channels assigned 01-10 [if mm = 00, number of channels equals number of receiver's voices]

3.3.7 **POLY MODE ON (ALL NOTES OFF)**
Bn 7F 00
n = Channel Number 0-F

4.0 SYSTEM MESSAGE SUMMARIES

4.1 SYSTEM COMMON MESSAGE HEX SUMMARIES

4.1.1 **<QUARTER FRAME> <Type/Data>**
F1 nd
n = Message Type 0-7
d = Message Data 0-F

4.1.2 **<SONG POSITION POINTER>**
<Pointer LSB>
<Pointer MSB>
F2 ll hh
ll = Song Position Pointer LSB 00-7F
hh = Song Position Pointer MSB 00-7F

4.1.3 **<SONG SELECT>**
<Song Number>
F3 ss
ss = Song Number 00-7F

4.1.4 **<TUNE REQUEST>**
F6

4.1.5 **<EOX>**
F7

4.2 SYSTEM REAL TIME MESSAGE HEX SUMMARIES

4.2.1 **<TIMING CLOCK>**
F8

4.2.2 **<START>**
FA

4.2.3 **<CONTINUE>**
FB

4.2.4 **<STOP>**
FC

4.2.5 **<ACTIVE SENSING>**
FE

4.2.6 **<SYSTEM RESET>**
FF

4.3 SYSTEM EXCLUSIVE MESSAGE HEX SUMMARIES

4.3.1 *MANUFACTURER SYSTEM EXCLUSIVE*
F0 aa ** F7
aa = Manufacturer ID (see *Specification Updates* for list)
** any number of Data Bytes with values of 00-7F

4.3.2 Universal Non-Real Time System Exclusive Format

F0 7E ** F7

** = any number of data bytes 00-7F

4.3.2.1 SAMPLE DUMP HEADER

F0 7E cc 01 ss ss ee ff ff ff gg gg gg hh hh hh ii ii ii jj F7

cc = Channel Number 00-7F
ss ss = Sample Number (LSB first)
ee = Sample Format 08-1C
ff ff ff = Sample Period (LSB first)
gg gg gg = Sample Length (LSB first)
hh hh hh = Sustain Loop Start Point (LSB first)
ii ii ii = Sustain Loop End Point (LSB first)
jj = Loop Type [00 = forwards only] [01= backwards/forwards]

4.3.2.2 SAMPLE DUMP DATA PACKET

F0 7E cc 02 kk sample data ll F7

cc = Channel Number 00-7F
kk = Running Packet Count 00-7F
sample data = 120 bytes of sample data 00-7F
ll = Checksum

4.3.2.3 DUMP REQUEST

F0 7E cc 03 ss ss F7

cc = Channel Number 00-7F
ss ss = Sample Requested (LSB first)

4.3.2.4 SET UP

FO 7E cc 04 st hr mn sc fr ff sl sm <additional info> F7

cc = Channel Number 00-7F
st = Set-up Type:
- 00 = Special
- 01 = Punch In Points
- 02 = Punch Out Points
- 03 = Delete Punch In Points
- 04 = Delete Punch Out Points
- 05 = Event Start Points
- 06 = Event Stop Points
- 07 = Event Start Points with additional info
- 08 = Event Stop Points with additional info
- 09 = Delete Event Start Point
- 0A = Delete Event Stop Point
- 0B = Cue Points
- 0C = Cue Points with additional info
- 0D = Delete Cue Point
- 0E = Event Name in additional info

hr = Hour and Type /(bit field: 0 yy zzzzz)
- yy = Type: 00 = 24 Frames/Second
  - 01 = 25 Frames/Second
  - 10 = 30 Frames/Second (drop frame)
  - 11 = 30 Frames/Second (non-drop frame)
- zzzzz = Hours: 00-17

mn = Minutes 00-3B
sc = Seconds 00-3B
fr = Frames 00-1D
ff = Fractional Frames 00-63
sl = Event Number (Special Type when Set-up Type is 00) LSB 00-7F
sm = Event Number (Special Type when Set-up Type is 00) MSB 00-7F

additional info = Event specific data bytes 00-7F

4.3.2.5 **WAIT**

F0 7E cc 7C pp F7

cc = Channel Number 00-7F

pp = Packet Number 00-7F

4.3.2.6 **CANCEL**

F0 7E cc 7D pp F7

cc = Channel Number 00-7F

pp = Packet Number 00-7F

4.3.2.7 **NAK**

F0 7E cc 7E pp F7

cc = Channel Number 00-7F

pp = Packet Number 00-7F

4.3.2.8 **ACK**

F0 7E cc 7F pp F7

cc = Channel Number 00-7F

pp = Packet Number 00-7F

4.3.3 Universal Real Time System Exclusive Format

F0 7F ** F7

** = any number of data bytes 00-7F

4.3.3.1 **FULL MESSAGE**

F0 7F 7F 01 00 hr mn sc fr F7

hr = Hour and Type (bit fields: 0 yy zzzzz)

yy = Type: 00 = 24 Frames/Second

01 = 25 Frames/Second

10 = 30 Frames/Second (drop frame)

11 = 30 Frames/Second (non-drop frame)

zzzzz = Hours: 00-17

mn = Minutes 00-3B

sc = Second 00-3B

fr = Frames 00-1D

4.3.3.2 **USER BITS**

F0 7F 7F 01 01 $0u_1$ $0u_2$ $0u_3$ $0u_4$ $0u_5$ $0u_6$ $0u_7$ $0u_8$ $0u_9$ F7

u_1-u_8 These 4-bit fields decode in an 8-bit format: $<u_1\ u_2><u_3u_4><u_5u_6><u_7u_8>$

u_9 = Format Code (bit field: 00ii)

4.3.4 Universal Non-Commercial System Exclusive Format

F0 7D ** F7

** = any number of data bytes 00-7F

Sample Dump Standard
Operation And Communication Details

Flowchart

(based on Sample Dump Standard)

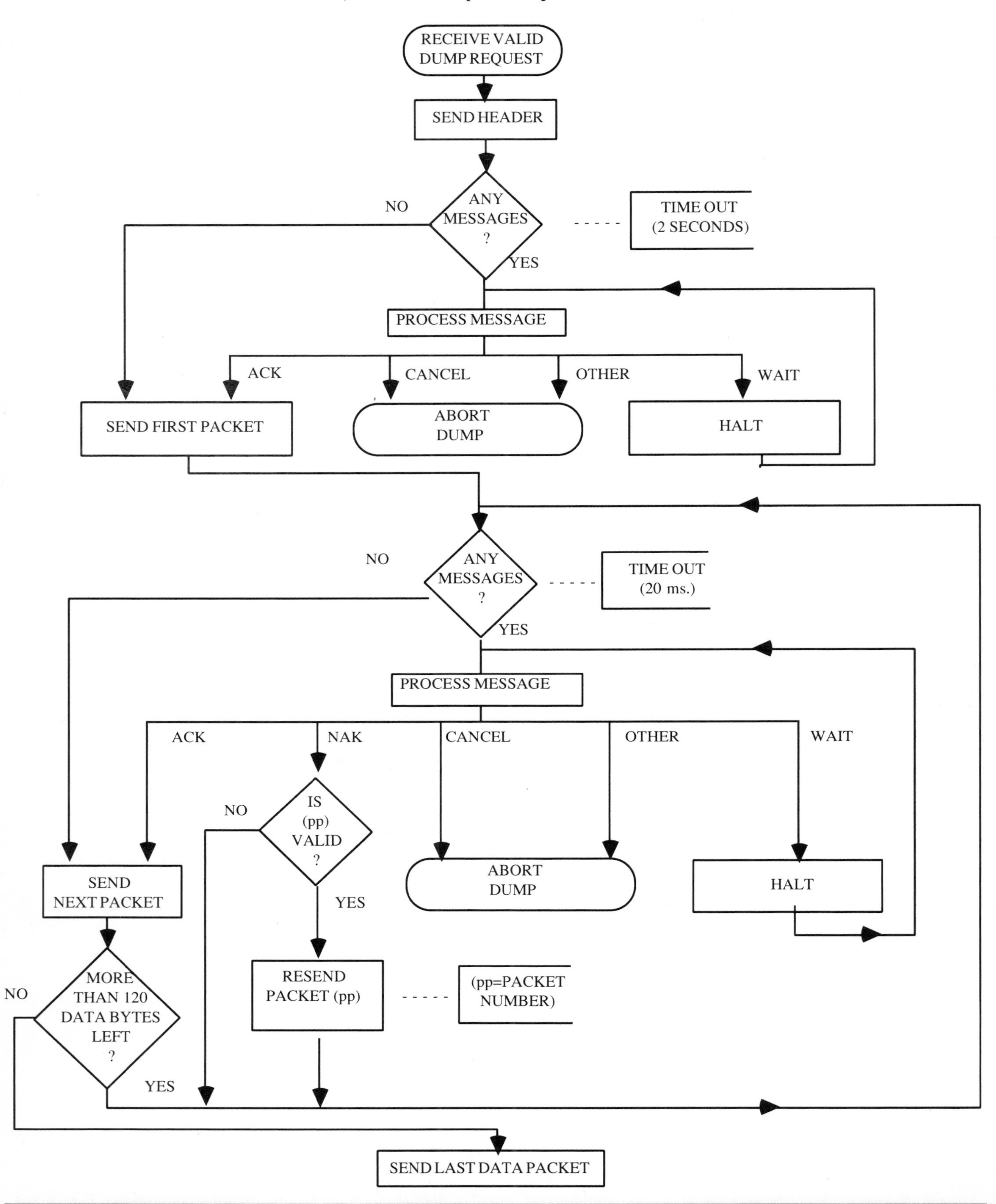

Sample Dump Communication Protocols

(based on examples in the Sample Dump Standard)

1.0 TIME OUTS

- Minimum TIME OUT after transmission of HEADER is 2 seconds.
- Minimum TIME OUT after transmission of DATA PACKET is 20 ms.

1.1 OPEN LOOP

Source Unit		Destination Unit
TIME OUT		(no message sent)
DATA PACKET	————————>	

If no message is received during a TIME OUT, an open loop is assumed and the next Data Packet is sent.

1.2 CLOSED LOOP

Source Unit		Destination Unit
TIME OUT	<————————	message

If a message is received during the TIME OUT (closed loop), the Source Unit acts on the message when it is received as shown below:

Source Unit		Destination Unit
Send next packet	<————————	**ACK**
	OR	
Resend packet	<————————	**NAK**
	OR	
Halt until next message	<————————	**WAIT**
	OR	
Abort dump	<————————	**CANCEL**
	OR	
Abort dump	<————————	Other message

2.0 SEND SAMPLE

2.1 OPEN LOOP

Source Unit		Destination Unit
HEADER	————————>	
TIME OUT (2 second min.)		
DATA PACKET	————————>	
TIME OUT (20 ms. min)		
DATA PACKET	————————>	
TIME OUT (20 ms. min)		
DATA PACKET	————————>	
	CONTINUE UNTIL ALL PACKETS SENT	

In an open loop the Source Unit sends all of the data packets with no handshaking.

2.2 CLOSED LOOP EXAMPLE A:

Source sample length < or = Destination sample length

Source Unit		Destination Unit
	<————————	**DUMP REQUEST**
HEADER	————————>	
TIME OUT	<————————	**ACK**
DATA PACKET	————————>	
TIME OUT	<————————	**ACK**
DATA PACKET	————————>	
TIME OUT	<————————	**ACK**
	<—CONTINUE—>	
last **DATA PACKET**	————————>	
TIME OUT	<————————	**ACK**
STOP		

In this closed loop example, handshaking is performed after each packet is accepted. Handshaking should follow transmission of the last packet to acknowledge no error occured when it was received.

2.3 CLOSED LOOP EXAMPLE B:

Source sample length > destination sample length

Source Unit		Destination Unit
	<————————	**DUMP REQUEST**
HEADER	————————>	
TIME OUT	<————————	**ACK**
DATA PACKET	————————>	
TIME OUT	<————————	**ACK**
DATA PACKET	————————>	
TIME OUT	<————————	**ACK**
	<—CONTINUE—>	
DATA PACKET	————————>	
TIME OUT	<————————	**CANCEL** (memory full)
ABORT		

In this example, the Destination Unit transmits CANCEL when its memory is full, telling the Source Unit not to send any more data packets.

2.4 CLOSED LOOP EXAMPLE C: NAK

	Source Unit		Destination Unit
		<————————	**DUMP REQUEST**
	HEADER	————————>	
	TIME OUT	<————————	**ACK**
	DATA PACKET	————————>	
	TIME OUT	<————————	**ACK**
	DATA PACKET	————————>	
	TIME OUT	<————————	**ACK**
	DATA PACKET	————————>	ERROR
	TIME OUT	<————————	**NAK**
resend	**DATA PACKET**	————————>	
	TIME OUT	<————————	**ACK**
next	**DATA PACKET**	————————>	
	TIME OUT	<————————	**ACK**
		CONTINUE UNTIL ALL PACKETS SENT	

When a reception error occurs, the Destination Unit transmits NAK, requesting that the last packet be resent. The Source Unit retransmits the packet requested by the NAK (if it is capable of doing so). After receiving an ACK for the resent packet, it continues with the dump.

2.5 CLOSED LOOP EXAMPLE D: WAIT

Source Unit		Destination Unit
	<————————	**DUMP REQUEST**
HEADER	————————>	
TIME OUT	<————————	**ACK**
DATA PACKET	————————>	
TIME OUT	<————————	**ACK**
DATA PACKET	————————>	
TIME OUT	<————————	**ACK**
DATA PACKET	————————>	
TIME OUT	<————————	**WAIT**
HALT		Disk Write
	<————————	**ACK**
DATA PACKET	————————>	
	CONTINUE UNTIL ALL PACKETS SENT	

If the Source Unit receives WAIT during a TIME OUT, it halts until another message is received. This frees the Destination Unit to perform any other tasks, such as disk write, etc. When the Destination Unit is ready to continue the dump, it sends an ACK as shown here. It could also stop the dump or request that a packet be resent by transmitting the appropriate CANCEL or NAK.

Application Notes For New Designers

The acceptance and continued development of MIDI has encouraged hardware and software engineers new to the music industry to design music technology products. Since **The Ferro MIDI Reference Series** provides a single source of all available implementation, System Exclusive, and communication protocol details, this series can be particularly useful to new designers. It provides a unique opportunity to get up-to-speed with the trends and practices currently employed by the Music Industry as a whole from a single source of information.

- If you are designing a product that must be compatible with those produced by another company, you'll gain valuable insight into the engineering philosophy of the target manufacturer by reviewing their published implementation and System Exclusive data.

- Engineers unfamiliar with the Music Industry design conventions can, from this single source, survey practices used by the industry as a whole.

- During the conceptual phase of the design cycle, use the implementation charts and System Exclusive listings to focus on interface capabilities, functions, and parameters required to make your products competitive with similar devices.

- A survey of MIDI data can provide insight to key design factors when analyzing the success or failure of a given product line.

- Analysis of the data, as a whole, can help identify potential new products by defining target areas not addressed by products currently on the market.

Converting Hex/Binary/Decimal MIDI Data Values

Depending on the source, MIDI data may be given as decimal, hex, or binary values. If you are not fluent with converting numbers between $base_{10}$, $base_{16}$, and $base_2$, use these tables to help you change from one numbering system to another.

Use *Table 1* to look up values 0 through 15 in hex, binary, and decimal, and *Table 2* to look up values 0 through 255 in hex and decimal.

CONVERTING 8-BIT BINARY VALUES TO 2-DIGIT HEX VALUES:

- Convert the leftmost 4 bits into the left hex digit. (Use *Table 1*.)
- Convert the rightmost 4 bits into the right hex digit. (Use *Table 1*.)

	LEFT BITS	RIGHT BITS		
binary 11110110 convert	**1111**	**0110**		
	F	**6**	=	**F6 hex**
	LEFT DIGIT	RIGHT DIGIT		

CONVERTING 2-DIGIT HEX VALUES TO 8-BIT BINARY VALUES:

- Convert the left hex digit into the leftmost 4 bits. (Use *Table 1*.)
- Convert the right hex digit into the rightmost 4 bits. (Use *Table 1*.)

	LEFT DIGIT	RIGHT DIGIT		
hex 5C convert	**5**	**C**		
	0101	**1100**	=	**01011100 binary**
	LEFT BITS	RIGHT BITS		

CONVERTING DECIMAL VALUES GREATER THAN 15 TO BINARY:

- Convert the decimal value to a 2-digit hex value. (Use *Table 2*.)
- Convert the hex value to an 8-bit binary value as described above.

	LEFT DIGIT	RIGHT DIGIT		
decimal 101 = hex 65 convert	**6**	**5**		
	0110	**0101**	=	**01100101 binary**
	LEFT BITS	RIGHT BITS		

CONVERTING AN 8-BIT BINARY VALUE TO A DECIMAL VALUE:

- Convert the binary value to a 2-digit hex value as described above.
- Convert the hex value to a decimal value. (Use *Table 2*.)

	LEFT BITS	RIGHT BITS		
binary 11111000 convert	**1111**	**1000**		
	F	**8**	=	**F8 hex = 248 decimal**
	LEFT DIGIT	RIGHT DIGIT		

Conversion Table 1

Hex	*Binary*	*Decimal*
0H	0 0 0 0	0
1H	0 0 0 1	1
2H	0 0 1 0	2
3H	0 0 1 1	3
4H	0 1 0 0	4
5H	0 1 0 1	5
6H	0 1 1 0	6
7H	0 1 1 1	7
8H	1 0 0 0	8
9H	1 0 0 1	9
AH	1 0 1 0	10
BH	1 0 1 1	11
CH	1 1 0 0	12
DH	1 1 0 1	13
EH	1 1 1 0	14
FH	1 1 1 1	15

Conversion Table 2

Decimal	*Hex*	*Decimal*	*Hex*	*Decimal*	*Hex*	*Decimal*	*Hex*
0	00H	32	20H	64	40H	96	60H
1	01H	33	21H	65	41H	97	61H
2	02H	34	22H	66	42H	98	62H
3	03H	35	23H	67	43H	99	63H
4	04H	36	24H	68	44H	100	64H
5	05H	37	25H	69	45H	101	65H
6	06H	38	26H	70	46H	102	66H
7	07H	39	27H	71	47H	103	67H
8	08H	40	28H	72	48H	104	68H
9	09H	41	29H	73	49H	105	69H
10	0AH	42	2AH	74	4AH	106	6AH
11	0BH	43	2BH	75	4BH	107	6BH
12	0CH	44	2CH	76	4CH	108	6CH
13	0DH	45	2DH	77	4DH	109	6DH
14	0EH	46	2EH	78	4EH	110	6EH
15	0FH	47	2FH	79	4FH	111	6FH
16	10H	48	30H	80	50H	112	70H
17	11H	49	31H	81	51H	113	71H
18	12H	50	32H	82	52H	114	72H
19	13H	51	33H	83	53H	115	73H
20	14H	52	34H	84	54H	116	74H
21	15H	53	35H	85	55H	117	75H
22	16H	54	36H	86	56H	118	76H
23	17H	55	37H	87	57H	119	77H
24	18H	56	38H	88	58H	120	78H
25	19H	57	39H	89	59H	121	79H
26	1AH	58	3AH	90	5AH	122	7AH
27	1BH	59	3BH	91	5BH	123	7BH
28	1CH	60	3CH	92	5CH	124	7CH
29	1DH	61	3DH	93	5DH	125	7DH
30	1EH	62	3EH	94	5EH	126	7EH
31	1FH	63	3FH	95	5FH	127	7FH

Conversion Table 2 (Continued)

Decimal	Hex	Decimal	Hex	Decimal	Hex	Decimal	Hex
128	80H	160	A0H	192	C0H	224	E0H
129	81H	161	A1H	193	C1H	225	E1H
130	82H	162	A2H	194	C2H	226	E2H
131	83H	163	A3H	195	C3H	227	E3H
132	84H	164	A4H	196	C4H	228	E4H
133	85H	165	A5H	197	C5H	229	E5H
134	86H	166	A6H	198	C6H	230	E6H
135	87H	167	A7H	199	C7H	231	E7H
136	88H	168	A8H	200	C8H	232	E8H
137	89H	169	A9H	201	C9H	233	E9H
138	8AH	170	AAH	202	CAH	234	EAH
139	8BH	171	ABH	203	CBH	235	EBH
140	8CH	172	ACH	204	CCH	236	ECH
141	8DH	173	ADH	205	CDH	237	EDH
142	8EH	174	AEH	206	CEH	238	EEH
143	8FH	175	AFH	207	CFH	239	EFH
144	90H	176	B0H	208	D0H	240	F0H
145	91H	177	B1H	209	D1H	241	F1H
146	92H	178	B2H	210	D2H	242	F2H
147	93H	179	B3H	211	D3H	243	F3H
148	94H	180	B4H	212	D4H	244	F4H
149	95H	181	B5H	213	D5H	245	F5H
150	96H	182	B6H	214	D6H	246	F6H
151	97H	183	B7H	215	D7H	247	F7H
152	98H	184	B8H	216	D8H	248	F8H
153	99H	185	B9H	217	D9H	249	F9H
154	9AH	186	BAH	218	DAH	250	FAH
155	9BH	187	BBH	219	DBH	251	FBH
156	9CH	188	BCH	220	DCH	252	FCH
157	9DH	189	BDH	221	DDH	253	FDH
158	9EH	190	BEH	222	DEH	254	FEH
159	9FH	191	BFH	223	DFH	255	FFH

Notes For Using System Exclusive Data

Devices use System Exclusive messages to perform functions not specifically defined by Channel Voice, Channel Mode, System Common, and System Real Time messages. Typically, they deal with data transfer and parameter control. Although their primary use is for factory-designed functions, the codes are published to allow others to make use of them as well. Many users are unaware of the creative potential implied by the existence of these messages.

For example, here is a list of instrument parameters that may be accessable via System Exclusive messages on many instruments that don't provide means of controlling them via Channel Voice messages.

- Filter Cut-Off
- Amplifier Gain
- Envelope Parameters
- Modulator/Carrier Tuning Ratios
- Chorus Rate and Speed
- Oscillator Level
- Waveform Select
- LFO Rate

If you have a MIDI control device that can be programmed to transmit System Exclusive messages (there are several such devices on the market), you can program it to control parameters such as those listed above (and others) from a keyboard, foot pedal, pitch wheel, or other performance controller. This kind of capability can, in effect, add an entire set of new performance features to a synthesizer or other MIDI instrument.*

You'll also find System Exclusive codes invaluable if you are writing MIDI programs for your personal computer. You'll find them particularly useful if you are creating software for any of the following applications:

- Voicing Programs for synthesizers or samplers
- Librarians for instruments, sequencers, or drum machines
- Sequencers
- Editors for sequencers and drum machines
- Computer composition software
- Music notation software
- MIDI "effects"

Of course, in order to use these messages in performance or programming applications, you must have a detailed listing of the messages and formats used. The messages are usually supplied as part of the user documentation that comes with a new instrument, and of course, **The MIDI System Exclusive Book** is a master source of all available System Exclusive codes.

***NOTE: For detailed suggestions and explanations on the creative use of parameters like those mentioned above, we recommend our synthesis course *Secrets of Analog and Digital Synthesis*.**

GENERAL APPLICATIONS

Implementation charts provide you with access to all major factors of a device's MIDI features. At a glance, you can learn such significant details about a MIDI device as:

- Which MIDI modes it supports
- What channels it receives and transmits on
- MIDI master controller functions
- MIDI slave functions
- Keyboard dynamics
- MIDI synchronization features
- Computer accessibility
- How well it can integrate into your MIDI system

The MIDI Implementation Book contains a comprehensive up-to-date collection of charts that can be used as a powerful and invaluable tool. For example, if you are looking for a new instrument, use the charts to sort through the MIDI features of similar devices. (You may be suprised to find that a more expensive device won't necessarily offer the MIDI features that are most important to you.) As your MIDI system grows and becomes more sophisticated, you'll be looking for MIDI devices that fit your particular applications. The charts are conveniently listed by application, allowing you to quickly locate devices that can solve your particular MIDI problems. Should you encounter an unfamiliar piece of MIDI gear at a session, chances are its implementation will be listed in **The MIDI Implementation Book**, and you can quickly find out what you need to know to make the unit work with you, not against you.

READING IMPLEMENTATION CHARTS

Of course, you must know how to read the charts and what the information they contain means, as well as how it can be put to use musically. If implementation charts are unfamiliar to you, this section will help to guide you through them. For technical details about the data in the charts, refer to the **MIDI 1.0 Specification** and **MIDI At A Glance** sections of this book.

GENERAL COMMENTS

Different symbols, spellings, etc. may be used to represent the same information from chart to chart. The Implementation charts in **The MIDI Implementation Book** have been standardized in this respect in order to present implementation details in a consistent manner. However, when you are comparing charts from owner's manuals, you may find the various conventions used by different manufacturers somewhat confusing. These variations are to be expected in a specification as young as MIDI. As MIDI matures, the representation of information on these charts will undoubtedly become more uniform. The following comments will guide you through some of the most common inconsistencies you may encounter when comparing charts from different sources.

- "O" and "X" symbols are used to indicate "Yes" or "No". The most common convention is to use "O" for "Yes". However, some charts use "X" for "Yes". Check the bottom right corner for a key explaining how the symbols are used.
- "OX" is often used to indicate a selectable function (one the user can enable/disable). However, selectability of a function is frequently not indicated, or may be mentioned in the *Remarks* or *Notes* areas.
- Some items may be meaningless in the context of certain devices, such as *Transmitted* information for a slave (receive only) device. In such cases "N/A" (not applicable) may be used. Other charts may show an "X", "–" (dash), or simply leave the space in question blank.
- MIDI modes should be listed by the numbers: Mode 1(OMNI ON, POLY), Mode 2 (OMNI ON, MONO), Mode 3 (OMNI OFF, POLY), and Mode 4 (OMNI OFF, MONO). The individual words "OMNI", "POLY", and "MONO" do not define any one of the four MIDI modes, but occasionally they are used (improperly) for that purpose. Typically, they are used to represent Modes 1, 3, and 4, but if you find these on a chart, you cannot be sure which mode (or modes) is being referred to. Check your owner's manual for more details.
- MIDI Mode messages may appear as OMNI ON, OMNI OFF, POLY ON, MONO ON, or in slightly abbreviated forms, OMNI ON/OFF, POLY, MONO.
- Hexadecimal values are usually indicated with the prefix "$" or the suffix "H"or "h".

*NOTE: If you want more application-oriented information on MIDI and how to use it, we recommend our book, ***The MIDI Book: Using MIDI and Related Interfaces***. If you would like to know more about how to creatively program and play synthesizers, we also recommend our course, ***The Secrets of Analog and Digital Synthesis.***

CHART SUMMARY

HEADER

- This area of the chart is where the *Manufacturer, Model*, and *Description* are given.
- Check the *Version* field on the chart and compare it to the version number of the piece of equipment you are using. If they are the same, then the chart should accurately reflect the device's MIDI features. If the device's version number is more recent than the chart's, it may have features not documented on the chart. If the chart's version number is more recent than the device's, some of the features described on the chart may not be implemented on the device. If this is the case, check with the manufacturer to find out how to upgrade the device to the latest version.

BASIC CHANNEL

- *Default* : This field tells you what channel the device transmits on and/or recognizes when it is first turned on. Many instruments allow the default channel to be changed by the user. This will be indicated here. For example, an instrument whose default channel can be set to any channel would show "1-16" or "All Channels" here.
- *Changed* : This field indicates which MIDI channels can be assigned by the user during operation.

MODE

- *Default* : This indicates which of the four MIDI modes is active when the unit is first powered-up. If the default mode can be changed, it will be indicated here.
- *Messages* : This field shows which of the four MIDI Mode messages are *Transmitted/Recognized* by the device. (Some charts may list modes here, not messages — see above.) Be aware that many instruments can be set manually to operate in different MIDI modes, even if they don't transmit/recognize mode messages.
- *Altered* : Only the *Recognized* column is valid for this entry. It is used to describe how a device will respond to a message requesting it to change to a mode it does not honor. For example, an instrument that does not operate in either of the two mono modes may treat the MONO message as an OMNI message in order to receive MIDI data. This will be indicated on the chart like this: "MONO ON —> OMNI ON" or "MONO —> OMNI".
- Some instruments may alter modes based on the value of the second data byte of the MONO mode message. (See *Channel Mode Message Summaries* in **MIDI At A Glance** for more details.) The value of this data is referred to as "M". Normally, this variable indicates how many mono channels a receiver should assign when it switches to a mono mode. Some devices that don't implement mono modes may switch to Mode 1 or Mode 3, depending on the value of M. This will be indicated on the chart with an expression like this:
  "MONO (M≠1) —> Mode 1, (M=1) —> Mode 3".

NOTE NUMBER

- *Transmitted* : The range of numbers given in this column show the actual MIDI Note Numbers transmitted by the device's keyboard (or other) controller. The range 21-108 corresponds to the 88 keys of a grand piano. If the range is greater than the number of keys on the unit, this generally indicates a MIDI transpose feature of some kind. Look to the *Remarks* column for more details.

- *Recognized* : There are two ranges of Note Numbers that may be given in this column. The first indicates the range of Note Numbers recognized by the device. Note Numbers outside of this range will be ignored (not played) by the device. (The maximum range of MIDI Note Numbers is 0-127.) The second range, labeled *True Voice*, indicates the range of notes the device can play. It is unnecessary to show this unless the *True Voice* range is less than the range of recognized Note Numbers. Recognized Note Numbers outside the *True Voice* range are shifted in octaves until they fall within the range.

Manufacturer
Example
[8 Voice Sampler]

Model
—
Version 2.0 Date 12/86

Function		Transmitted	Recognized	Remarks
BASIC CHANNEL	Default	1	1	
	Changed	1-16	1-16	
MODE	Default	1	1	Honors Modes 1,3
	Messages	X	OMNI ON/OFF	
	Altered			
NOTE NUMBER		36-96	36-96	
	True Voice			
VELOCITY	Note On	O	O	
	Note Off	X	X	
TOUCH	Key's	X	X	
	Chan's	OX	OX	
PITCH BENDER		OX	OX	
CONTROL CHANGE	Left Wheel	OX	OX	assignable to controllers 0-31
	Right Wheel	OX	OX	
	Pedal	OX	OX	
	Sustain Pedal	OX	OX	
PROGRAM CHANGE		0-98	0-98	
	True #		1-99	
SYSTEM EXCLUSIVE		X	X	
SYSTEM COMMON	Song Pos	X	X	
	Song Sel	X	X	
	Tune	X	X	
SYSTEM REAL TIME	Clock	O	OX	recognition of commands is selectable
	Messages	Start, Stop	Start, Stop	
AUX	Local Control	X	O	
	All Notes Off	X	O (123-127)	
	Active Sense		X	
	Reset	O	X	
NOTES:				

Mode 1 : OMNI ON, POLY Mode 2 : OMNI ON, MONO O : Yes
Mode 3 : OMNI OFF, POLY Mode 4: OMNI OFF, MONO X : No

Manufacturer | Model

Version | Date

Function		Transmitted	Recognized	Remarks
BASIC CHANNEL	Default Changed			
MODE	Default Messages Altered			
NOTE NUMBER	True Voice			
VELOCITY	Note On Note Off			
TOUCH	Key's Chan's			
PITCH BENDER				
CONTROL CHANGE				
PROGRAM CHANGE	True #			
SYSTEM EXCLUSIVE				
SYSTEM COMMON	Song Pos Song Sel Tune			
SYSTEM REAL TIME	Clock Messages			
AUX	Local Control All Notes Off Active Sense Reset			
NOTES:				

Mode 1 : OMNI ON, POLY
Mode 3 : OMNI OFF, POLY
Mode 2 : OMNI ON, MONO
Mode 4: OMNI OFF, MONO
O : Yes
X : No

VELOCITY

- *Note On :* This will tell you if the unit transmits or recognizes **variable** velocity data. The maximum range of velocities is 1-127 (01-7FH). Some devices only transmit and/or recognize a subset of this range. Some drum machines, for example, transmit only two values, one for "normal" dynamics and another for "accents". In general, if the range is less than the full range, the details will be shown here. For instance, "v = 40H Normal, v = 7FH Accent". If no range is given, it is usually safe to assume that the full range of velocities is transmitted and/or recognized.
- *Note Off* : Similar to *Note On* except it details if and how a device transmits and/or recognizes Note Off velocities. Many instruments transmit "Note On, v = 0" as an alternative to the implicit Note Off message. If this is the case, it will often be indicated by showing the hex code for the Note On message in the *Transmitted* column. For example, "9nH v=0" or "$9n00".

AFTER TOUCH

- *Key's* : This indicates if the device transmits/recognizes Polyphonic Key Pressure messages (independent pressure values for each key).
- *Chan's* : This indicates if the device transmits/recognizes Channel Pressure messages (one pressure value for the channel).

PITCH BENDER

- Along with indicating if the unit transmits/recognizes Pitch Wheel Change Messages, the *Remarks* column will often give details on the resolution and range of the bender.

CONTROL CHANGE

- *Transmitted* : This column will list the Controller Numbers transmitted by the device's on-board controllers. (See *MIDI Controller Definitions* in **Specification Updates**)
- *Recognized* : The mapping of MIDI controller numbers to on-board parameters is detailed in this column. (See *MIDI Controller Definitions* in **Specification Updates**)

PROGRAM CHANGE

- *Transmitted* : The range of Program Numbers transmitted by the device is shown here. The maximum range is 0-127 (00-7FH).
- *Recognized* : The range of recognized Program Numbers is given here. The actual numbers they correspond to on the particular unit are shown as the *True #* range.

SYSTEM EXCLUSIVE*

- The *Transmitted/Recognized* columns will indicate if System Exclusive messages are generated or recognized by the unit. The *Remarks* column should give details about what kinds of messages and how they are used. The owner's manual should give details about the specific messages and their formats.

SYSTEM COMMON

- The unit's ability to transmit/recognize Song Position, Song Select, and Tune Request messages is given here.

SYSTEM REAL TIME

- *Clock* : Transmission of the MIDI Clock message indicates that a device can be used as a master controller in a MIDI synchronized system. Recognition of Clock messages means the device can be "slaved" to an external source of MIDI clock messages.
- *Messages* : The Real Time messages are Stop, Start, and Continue. If they are transmitted/recognized by the unit, it will be indicated here along with a list of the particular messages utilized.

AUX MESSAGES

- This section of the chart tells you how a device handles *Local Control, All Notes Off, Active Sensing,* and *System Reset* messages.

*NOTE: Implementation Charts in ***The MIDI Implementation Book*** are marked with this symbol " ✣ " to indicate that detailed System Exclusive listings for the device are contained in ***The MIDI System Exclusive Book.***

Filling Out MIDI Implementation Charts

Many of the entries on an implementation chart can be represented with different symbols, spellings, etc. Although each of these variations is technically correct, the overall effectiveness of the charts would be enhanced if items were represented in a consistent manner from chart to chart. We recommend the following conventions. They conform with MMA guidelines and, for the most part, reflect the common usage in the majority of charts that have been generated by MIDI manufacturers. The charts in **The MIDI Implementation Book** follow these guidelines.

GENERAL COMMENTS

- Refer to MIDI modes by number. For example "Mode 3", "Modes 1, 3, 4", etc.

- Mode messages are spelled in UPPER CASE letters with the following format: OMNI ON, OMNI OFF, MONO, POLY. OMNI ON/OFF may also be used.

- Use "O" for "Yes" and "X" for "No". "OX" can be used to indicate a selectable feature. (The user can enable/disable transmission and or recognition.)

- Use "N/A" for "not applicable".

- Indicate hex values with "H", as in "9nH".

- When entering information for functions with multiple items, such as *System Common* or *Aux Messages*, don't leave any items blank. Each should have an "O", "X", "OX", or "N/A". The only exception to this should be when an entire function is not applicable to a device, in which case a single "N/A" centered in the box would suffice. This could be done, for example, in each of the *Transmitted* boxes of a slave-only device.

- Whenever possible, use the *Remarks* boxes for comments referencing items in that function row and *Notes* for more general comments.

- Avoid putting comments in the *Transmitted* or *Recognized* columns. Use an asterisk ("*") to reference comments in *Remarks* or *Notes* instead.

CHART SUMMARY

HEADER

- The *Manufacturer, Model, and Description* fields in the chart's header are self explanatory. Make sure to enter the *Date* and *Version* that are applicable for the implementation described in the chart.
- If *Version* is not applicable, enter a dash "—" in the field. Avoid leaving any fields (except *Remarks* or *Notes*) blank.

BASIC CHANNEL

- Indicate channels with numbers only. Use "1-16" to indicate "All Channels".
- *Default* : Show the Channel Number(s) the device defaults to on power-up.
- *Changed* : Show the Channel Number(s) the device can be assigned to transmit and receive on.

MODE

- *Default* : Show the default mode(s) using the numerical format, "Mode 1", etc.
- *Messages* : List the mode **messages** (OMNI ON/OFF, POLY, MONO) transmitted/recognized by the device. If mode messages are recognized as All Notes Off messages only (in other words, they have no effect on the receiver's operational mode), put an "X" in the *Recognized* column and list the decimal code for the messages in the *All Notes Off* entry in the *AUX MESSAGES* section of the chart.
- *Altered* : Only entries in the *Recognized* column are valid for this item. Take care to differentiate MIDI Modes from the variable "M". For example, MONO (M ≠ 1) —>Mode 1, (M = 1) —> Mode 3.
- *Remarks* : List the modes honored by the device here. For example, "Honors Modes 3, 4".

NOTE NUMBER

- List the transmitted/recognized note numbers as a decimal range.
- *True Voice* : Only entries in the*Recognized* column are valid for this item. Enter a range here only if it is **different** than the range of recognized Note Numbers given.

VELOCITY

- *Note On* : Enter an "O" here only if the device transmits and/or recognizes **variable** Note On velocity data. If the range is less than the maximum defined range of 1-127 it may be shown here. For example "v=1-120" or "v = 40H Normal, v = 7FH Accent".
- *Note Off* : Enter an "O" here only if the device transmits and/or recognizes **variable** Note Off velocity data. If the device transmits the "Note On v = 0" version of the Note Off message, show it by entering "9nH (v=0)" in the *Transmitted* column. (Since all MIDI devices must recognize this form of Note Off, there is no need to show it in the *Recognized* column.)

AFTER TOUCH

- *Key's* : Use "O", "X", "OX", or "N/A" to indicate if Polyphonic Key Pressure messages are *Transmitted* and/or *Recognized* .
- *Chan's* : Use "O", "X", "OX", or "N/A" to indicate if Channel Pressure messages are *Transmitted* and/or *Recognized.*

PITCH BENDER

- Use "O", "X", "OX", or "N/A" to indicate if Pitch Wheel Change messages are *Transmitted* and/or *Recognized.* Indicate resolution and range in *Remarks.*

CONTROL CHANGE

- To show a list of controllers, list the Controller Numbers (in decimal format) and their descriptions down the right side of the *Function* column. Show an "O", "X", or "OX" for each controller in the *Transmitted* and *Recognized* columns. Use the *Remarks* column for comments.

PROGRAM CHANGE

- If the device transmits and/or recognizes Program Change messages, don't use just an "O" symbol. Instead, indicate the transmitted and/or recognized Program Numbers as a range of decimal values.
- *True #* : Only entries in the *Recognized* column are valid for this item. Enter a range here only if it is **different** than the range of recognized Program Numbers.

SYSTEM COMMON

- *Song Pos* : Use "O", "X", "OX", or "N/A" to indicate if Song Position messages are *Transmitted* and/or *Recognized* .
- *Song Sel*: : If the device transmits and/or recognizes Song Select messages, don't use just an "O" symbol. Instead, indicate the *Transmitted/Recognized* Song Numbers as a range of decimal values.
- *Tune* : Use "O", "X", "OX", or "N/A" to indicate if Tune message is *Transmitted* and/or *Recognized* .

SYSTEM REAL TIME

- *Clock* : Use "O", "X", "OX", or "N/A" to indicate if the MIDI Clock message is *Transmitted* and/or *Recognized.*
- *Messages* : If the device transmits and/or recognizes Real Time messages, don't use just an "O" symbol. Instead, indicate the *Transmitted/Recognized* messages (Start, Stop, Continue).

AUX MESSAGE

- *Local Control* : Use "O", "X", "OX", or "N/A" to indicate if Local Control message is *Transmitted* and/or *Recognized* .
- *All Notes Off* : If the device transmits and/or recognizes All Notes Off messages, don't use just an "O" symbol. Instead, list the decimal values (123—127) *Transmitted* and/or *Recognized* .
- *Active Sense* : Use "O", "X", "OX", or "N/A" to indicate if Active Sensing messages are *Transmitted* and/or *Recognized.*
- *Reset* : Use "O", "X", "OX", or "N/A" to indicate if Reset message is *Transmitted* and/or *Recognized.*

SECTION 3: SPECIFICATION DETAILS

In this section:

MIDI 1.0 Specification

• Outline
This outline details the major topics presented in the MIDI 1.0 Specification. It also provides a quick reference for finding specific details within the specification.
• The Specification
The complete MIDI 1.0 specification. Topics have been numbered to cross reference with the outline.

MIDI 1.0 Specification Updates

• Manufacturer ID Codes
Up-to-date listings of all permanent and temporary assigned Manufacturer ID codes.
• MIDI Controller Definitions
Up-to-date listing of all defined Controller Numbers.
• Using Registered and Non-Registered Parameters
Design guidelines for devices using Registered and/or Non-Registered Parameters.
• System Exclusive Extensions
Several extensions have been added to the original System Exclusive format. The new formats and messages are described in detail.

Sample Dump Standard

• Overview
Description of data and message formats used by the Sample Dump Standard
• The Standard
The complete Sample Dump Standard document

MIDI Time Code Specification

• Overview
• Detailed Specification

Manufacturer's System Exclusive Formats

• Introduction to System Exclusive Formats
• Akai Exclusive Formats
• Casio Exclusive Formats
• Kawai Exclusive Formats
• Korg Exclusive Formats
• Roland Exclusive Formats
• Yamaha Exclusive Formats

Terminology Guide

Important terms cross-referenced between this and other **FERRO** books.

MIDI 1.0 Specification: Outline

1.0 INTRODUCTION

2.0 CONVENTIONS

3.0 HARDWARE
- 3.1 (Transmission)
- 3.2 (Circuit)
- 3.3 (Connectors)
- 3.4 (Cables)
- 3.5 (MIDI THRU)

4.0 DATA FORMAT
- 4.1 MESSAGE TYPES
  - 4.1.1 Channel
    - 4.1.1.1 Voice (TABLE II)
    - 4.1.1.2 Mode (TABLE III)
  - 4.1.2 System
    - 4.1.2.1 Common (TABLE IV)
    - 4.1.2.2 Real Time (TABLE V)
    - 4.1.2.3 Exclusive (TABLE VI)
- 4.2 DATA TYPES
  - 4.2.1 Status Bytes (TABLE I)
    - 4.2.1.1 Running Status
    - 4.2.1.2 Unimplemented Status
    - 4.2.1.3 Undefined Status
  - 4.2.2 Data Bytes
- 4.3 CHANNEL MODES
  - 4.3.1 (Definitions)
  - 4.3.2 (Restrictions)

5.0 POWER-UP DEFAULT CONDITIONS

6.0 TABLES
- 6.1 TABLE I: SUMMARY OF STATUS BYTES
- 6.2 TABLE II: CHANNEL VOICE MESSAGES
- 6.3 TABLE III: CHANNEL MODE MESSAGES
- 6.4 TABLE IV: SYSTEM COMMON MESSAGES
- 6.5 TABLE V: SYSTEM REAL TIME MESSAGES
- 6.6 TABLE VI: SYSTEM EXCLUSIVE MESSAGES

MIDI 1.0 Specification *

1.0 INTRODUCTION

MIDI is the acronym for Musical Instrument Digital Interface.

MIDI enables synthesizers, sequencers, home computers, rhythm machines, etc. to be interconnected through a standard interface.

Each MIDI-equipped instrument usually contains a receiver and a transmitter. Some instruments may contain only a receiver or transmitter. The receiver receives messages in MIDI format and executes MIDI commands. It consists of an optoisolator, Universal Asynchronous Receiver-Transmitter (UART), and other hardware needed to perform the intended functions. The transmitter originates messages in MIDI format, and transmits them by way of a UART and line driver.

The MIDI standard hardware and data format are defined in this specification.

2.0 CONVENTIONS

Status and Data bytes given in Tables I through VI are given in binary.

Numbers followed by an "H" are in hexadecimal.

All other numbers are in decimal.

3.0 HARDWARE

3.1 The interface operates at 31.25 (+/- 1%) Kbaud, asynchronous, with a start bit, 8 data bits (D0 to D7), and a stop bit. This makes a total of 10 bits for a period of 320 microseconds per serial byte.

3.2 Circuit: See Figure 1. 5 mA current loop type. Logical 0 is current ON. One output shall drive one and only one input. The receiver shall be optoisolated and require less than 5 mA to turn on. Sharp PC-900 and HP 6N138 optoisolators have been found acceptable. Other high-speed optoisolators may be satisfactory. Rise and fall times should be less than 2 microseconds.

3.3 Connectors: DIN 5-pin (180 degree) female panel-mount receptacle. An example is the SWITCHCRAFT 57GB5F. The connectors shall be labelled "MIDI IN" and "MIDI OUT". Note that pins 1 and 3 are not used, and should be left unconnected in the receiver and transmitter.

3.4 Cables shall have a maximum length of fifty feet (15 meters), and shall be terminated on each end by a corresponding 5-pin DIN male plug, such as the SWITCHCRAFT 05GM5M. The cable shall be shielded twisted pair, with the shield connected to pin 2 at both ends.

3.5 A "MIDI THRU" output may be provided if needed, which provides a direct copy of data coming in MIDI IN. For very long chain lengths (more than three instruments), higher-speed optoisolators must be used to avoid additive rise/fall time errors, which affect pulse width duty cycle.

* NOTE: This is the complete MIDI 1.0 specification. In order to make the specification more accessable, we have numbered the major topics so they can be referenced from the preceding outline. Aside from the addition of these numbers, no changes or alterations have been made to the specification. It is reproduced here in its entirety.

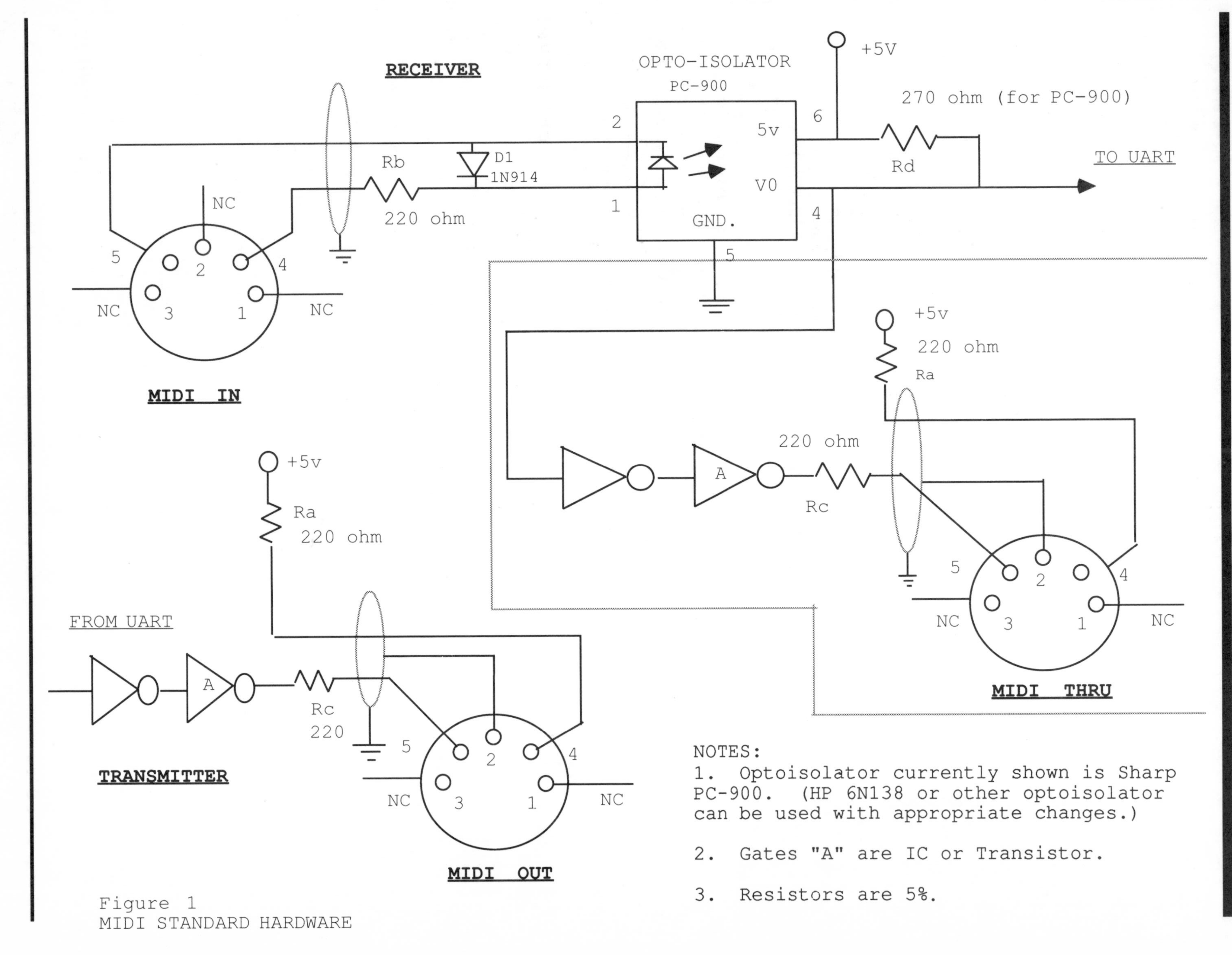

NOTES:
1. Optoisolator currently shown is Sharp PC-900. (HP 6N138 or other optoisolator can be used with appropriate changes.)

2. Gates "A" are IC or Transistor.

3. Resistors are 5%.

Figure 1
MIDI STANDARD HARDWARE

4.0 DATA FORMAT

All MIDI communication is achieved through multi-byte "messages" consisting of one Status byte followed by one or two Data bytes, except Real-Time and Exclusive messages (see below).

4.1 MESSAGE TYPES

Messages are divided into two main categories: Channel and System.

4.1.1 Channel

Each channel message contains a 4-bit number in the Status byte, which addresses the message specifically to one of 16 channels. These messages are thereby intended for any units in a system whose channel numbers match the channel number encoded into the Status byte.

There are two types of Channel messages: Voice and Mode.

4.1.1.1 Voice

To control the instrument's voices, Voice messages are sent over the Voice Channels.

4.1.1.2 Mode

To define the instrument's response to Voice messages, Mode messages are sent over the instrument's Basic Channel.

4.1.2 System

System messages are not encoded with channel numbers.

There are three types of System messages: Common, Real-Time, and Exclusive.

4.1.2.1 Common

Common messages are intended for all units in a system.

4.1.2.2 Real-Time

Real-Time messages are intended for all units in a system. They contain Status bytes only—no Data bytes. Real-Time messages may be sent at any time—even between bytes of a message that has a different status. In such cases the Real-Time message is either ignored or acted upon, after which the receiving process resumes under the previous status.

4.1.2.3 Exclusive

Exclusive messages can contain any number of Data bytes, and are terminated by an End of Exclusive (EOX) or any other Status byte. These messages include a Manufacturer's Identification (ID) code. If the receiver does not recognize the ID code, it should ignore the ensuing data.

4.2 DATA TYPES

4.2.1 Status Bytes

Status Bytes are 8-bit binary numbers in which the Most Significant Bit (MSB) is set (binary 1). Status bytes serve to identify the message type, that is, the purpose of the Data bytes that follow the Status byte.

Except for Real-Time messages, new Status bytes will always command the receiver to adopt their status, even if the new Status is received before the last message was completed.

4.2.1.1 Running Status

For Voice and Mode messages only, when a Status byte is received and processed, the receiver will remain in that status until a different Status is received. Therefore, if the same Status byte would be repeated, it may (optionally) be omitted so that only the correct number of Data bytes need be sent. Under Running Status, then a complete message need only consist of specified Data bytes sent in the specified order.

The Running Status feature is especially useful for communicating long strings of Note On/Off messages, where "Note On with Velocity Off" is used for Note Off. (A separate Note Off Status byte is also available.)

Running Status will be stopped when any other Status byte intervenes, except that Real-Time messages will only interrupt the Running Status temporarily.

4.2.1.2 Unimplemented Status

Any Status bytes received for functions that the receiver has not implemented should be ignored, and subsequent data bytes ignored.

4.2.1.3 Undefined Status

Undefined Status bytes must not be used. Care should be taken to prevent illegal messages from being sent during power-up or power-down. If undefined Status bytes are received, they should be ignored, as should subsequent Data bytes.

4.2.2 Data Bytes

Following the Status byte, there are (except for Real-Time messages) one or two Data bytes, which carry the content of the message. Data bytes are 8-bit binary numbers in which the MSB is reset (binary 0). The number and range of Data bytes that must follow each Status byte are specified in the tables that follow. Inside the receiver, action on the message should wait until all Data bytes required under the current status are received. Receivers should ignore Data bytes that have not been properly preceded by a valid Status byte (with the exception of "Running Status," above).

4.3 CHANNEL MODES

Synthesizers contain sound generation elements called voices. Voice assignment is the algorithmic process of routing Note On/Off data from the keyboard to the voices so that the musical notes are correctly played with accurate timing.

4.3.1 When MIDI is implemented, the relationship between the 16 available MIDI channels and the synthesizer's voice assignment must be defined. Several Mode messages are available for this purpose (see Table III). They are Omni (On/Off), Poly, and Mono. Poly and Mono are mutually exclusive, i. e., Poly Select disables Mono, and vice versa. Omni, when on, enables the receiver to receive Voice messages in all Voice Channels without discrimination. When Omni is off, the receiver will accept Voice messages from only the selected Voice Channel(s).

Mono, when on, restricts the assignment of Voices to just one voice per Voice Channel (Monophonic). When Mono is off (=Poly On), any number of voices may be allocated by the Receiver's normal voice assignment algorithm (Polyphonic). For a receiver assigned to Basic Channel "N", the four possible modes arising from the two Mode messages are:

Mode	**Omni**		
1	On	Poly	Voice messages are received from all Voice Channels, and assigned to voices polyphonically.
2	On	Mono	Voice messages are received from all Voice Channels, and control only one voice, monophonically.
3	Off	Poly	Voice messages are received in Voice Channel N only, and are assigned to voices polyphonically.
4	Off	Mono	Voice messages are received in Voice Channels N through N+M-1, and assigned monophonically to voices 1 through M, respectively. The number of voices M is specified by the third byte of the Mono Mode Message.

Four modes are applied to transmitters (also assigned to Basic Channel N). Transmitters with no channel selection capability will normally transmit on Basic Channel 1 (N=0).

Mode	**Omni**		
1	On	Poly	All voice messages are transmitted in Channel N.
2	On	Mono	Voice messages for one voice are sent in Channel N.
3	Off	Poly	Voice messages for all voices are sent in Channel N.
4	Off	Mono	Voice messages for voices 1 through M are transmitted in Voice Channels N through N+M-1, respectively. (Single voice per channel.)

4.3.2 A MIDI receiver or transmitter can operate under one and only one mode at a time. Usually the receiver and transmitter will be in the same mode. If a mode cannot be honored by the receiver, it may ignore the message (and any subsequent data bytes), or it may switch to an alternate mode (usually Mode 1, Omni On/Poly).

Mode messages will be recognized by a receiver only when sent in the Basic Channel to which the receiver has been assigned, regardless of the current mode. Voice messages may be received in the Basic Channel and in other channels (which are all called Voice Channels) that are related specifically to the Basic Channel by the rules above, depending on which mode has been selected.

A MIDI receiver may be assigned to one or more Basic Channels by default or by user control. For example, an eight-voice synthesizer might be assigned to Basic Channel 1 on power-up. The user could then switch the instrument to be configured as two four-voice synthesizers, each assigned to its own Basic Channel. Separate Mode messages would then be sent to each four-voice synthesizer, just as if they were physically separate instruments.

5.0 POWER-UP DEFAULT CONDITIONS

On power-up all instruments should default to Mode #1. Except for Note On/Off Status, all Voice messages should be disabled. Spurious or undefined transmissions must be suppressed.

TABLE I
SUMMARY OF STATUS BYTES

STATUS D7---D0	# OF DATA BYTES	DESCRIPTION
Channel Voice Messages		
1000nnnn	2	Note Off event
1001nnnn	2	Note On event (velocity = 0:Note Off)
1010nnnn	2	Polyphonic key pressure/after touch
1011nnnn	2	Control change
1100nnnn	1	Program change
1101nnnn	1	Channel pressure/after touch
1110nnnn	2	Pitch wheel change
Channel Mode Messages		
1011nnnn	2	Selects Channel Mode
System Messages		
11110000	*****	System Exclusive
11110sss	0 to 2	System Common
11111ttt	0	System Real Time

Notes:

nnnn:	N-1, where N = Channel #, i.e., 0000 is Channel 1. 0001 is Channel 2. . . . 1111 is Channel 16.
*****:	0iiiiiii, data, ..., EOX
iiiiiii:	Identification
sss:	1 to 7
ttt:	0 to 7

TABLE II
CHANNEL VOICE MESSAGES

STATUS	DATA BYTES	DESCRIPTION
1000nnnn	0kkkkkkk 0vvvvvvv	Note Off (see notes 1-4) vvvvvvv: note off velocity
1001nnnn	0kkkkkkk 0vvvvvvv	Note On (see notes 1-4) vvvvvvv ≠ 0: velocity vvvvvvv = 0: note off
1010nnnn	0kkkkkkk 0vvvvvvv	Polyphonic Key Pressure (After-Touch) vvvvvvv: pressure value
1011nnnn	0ccccccc 0vvvvvvv	Control Change ccccccc: control # (0-121)(see notes 5-8) vvvvvvv: control value ccccccc = 122 thru 127: Reserved. See Table III
1100nnnn	0ppppppp	Program Change ppppppp: program number (0-127)
1101nnnn	0vvvvvvv	Channel Pressure (After-Touch) vvvvvvv: pressure value
1110nnnn	0vvvvvvv 0vvvvvvv	Pitch Wheel Change LSB (see note 10) Pitch Wheel Change MSB

NOTES:

1. nnnn: Voice Channel # (1-16, coded as defined in Table I notes)
2. kkkkkkk: note # (0 - 127)
   kkkkkkk = 60: Middle C of keyboard

   0 12 24 36 48 60 72 84 96 108 120 127

   ac c c c c c c c
   +-------------------piano range---------------------------+

3. vvvvvvv: key velocity
   A logarithmic scale would be advisable.

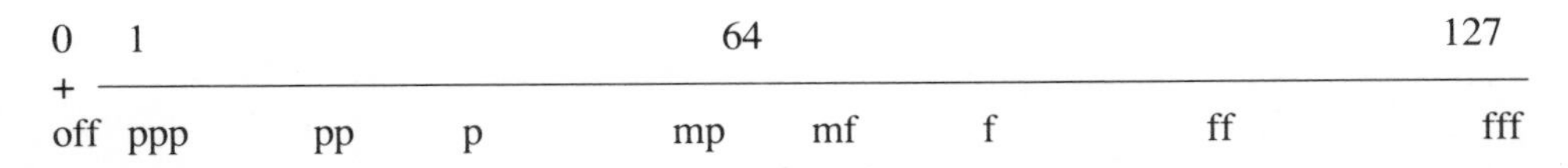

   vvvvvvv = 64: in case of no velocity sensors
   vvvvvvv = 0: Note Off, with velocity = 64

4. Any Note On message sent should be balanced by sending a Note Off message for that note in that channel at some later time.

5. ccccccc: control number

ccccccc	Description
0	Continuous Controller 0 MSB
1	Continuous Controller 1 MSB (MODULATION WHEEL)
2	Continuous Controller 2 MSB
3	Continuous Controller 3 MSB
4-31	Continuous Controllers 4-31 MSB
32	Continuous Controller 0 LSB
33	Continuous Controller 1 LSB (MODULATION WHEEL)
34	Continuous Controller 2 LSB
35	Continuous Controller 3 LSB
36-63	Continuous Controllers 4-31 LSB
64-95	Switches (On/Off)
96-121	Undefined
122-127	Reserved for Channel Mode messages (see Table III)

6. The controllers are not specifically defined. A manufacturer can assign the logical controllers to physical ones as necessary. The controller allocation table must be provided in the user's operation manual.

7. Continuous controllers are divided into Most Significant and Least Significant Bytes. If only seven bits of resolution are needed for any particular controllers, only the MSB is sent. It is not necssary to send the LSB. If more resolution is needed, then both are sent: first the MSB, then the LSB. If only the LSB has changed in value, the LSB may be sent without re-sending the MSB.

8. vvvvvvv: control value (MSB)

(for controllers)

0 + min ———————— 127 + max

(for switches)

0 + off ———————— 127 + on

Numbers 1 through 126, inclusive, are ignored.

9. Any messages (e.g. Note On), which are sent successively under the same status, can be sent without a Status Byte until a different Status byte is needed.

10. Sensitivity of the pitch bender is selected in the receiver. Center position value (no pitch change) is 2000H, which would be transmitted EnH-00H-40H.

TABLE III
CHANNEL MODE MESSAGES

STATUS	DATA BYTES	DESCRIPTION
1011nnnn	0ccccccc 0vvvvvvv	Mode Messages ccccccc = 122: Local Control vvvvvvv = 0, Local Control Off vvvvvvv = 127, Local Control On ccccccc = 123: All Notes Off vvvvvvv = 0 ccccccc = 124: Omni Mode Off (All Notes Off) vvvvvvv = 0 ccccccc = 125: Omni Mode On (All Notes Off) vvvvvvv = 0 ccccccc = 126: Mono Mode On (Poly Mode Off) (All Notes Off) vvvvvvv = M, where M is the number of channels. vvvvvvv = 0, the number of channels equals the number of voices in the receiver. ccccccc = 127: Poly Mode On (Mono Mode Off) vvvvvvv = 0 (All Notes Off)

NOTES:

1. nnnn: Basic Channel # (1-16, coded as defined in Table I)

2. Messages 123 thru 127 function as All Notes Off Messages. They will turn off all voices controlled by the assigned Basic Channel. Except for message 123, All Notes Off, they should not be sent periodically, but only for a specific purpose. In no case should they be used in lieu of Note Off commands to turn off notes which have been previously turned on.. Therefore, any All Notes Off commands (123-127) may be ignored by receiver with no possibility of notes staying on, since any Note On command must have a corresponding specific Note Off command.

3. Control Change #122, Local Control, is optionally used to interupt the internal control path between the keyboard, for example, and the sound-generating circuitry. If 0 (Local Off message) is received, the path is disconnected: the keyboard data goes only to MIDI, and the sound-generating circuitry is controlled only by incoming MIDI data. If a 7FH (Local On message) is received, normal operation is restored.

4. The third byte of "Mono" specifies the number of channels in which Monophonic Voice messages are to be sent. This number, "M", is a number between 1 and 16. The channel(s) being used, then, will be the current Basic Channel (=N) through N+M-1 up to a maximum of 16. If M=0, this is a special case directing the receiver to assign all its voices, one per channel, from the Basic channel N through 16.

TABLE IV
SYSTEM COMMON MESSAGES

STATUS	DATA BYTES	DESCRIPTION
11110001		Undefined
11110010		Song Position Pointer
	0lllllll	lllllll: (Least significant)
	0hhhhhhh	hhhhhhh: (Most significant)
11110011	0sssssss	Song Select sssssss: Song #
11110100		Undefined
11110101		Undefined
11110110	none	Tune Request
11110111	none	EOX: "End of System Exclusive" flag

NOTES:

1. Song Position Pointer: is an internal register that holds the number of MIDI beats (1 beat = 6 MIDI clocks) since the start of the song. Normally it is set to 0 when the START switch is pressed, which starts sequence playback. It then increments with every sixth MIDI clock receipt, until STOP is pressed. If CONTINUE is pressed, it continues to increment. It can be arbitrarily preset (to a resolution of 1 beat) by the SONG POSITION POINTER message.

2. Song Select: Specifies which song or sequence is to be played upon receipt of a Start (Real-Time) message.

3. Tune Request: Used with analog synthesizers to request them to tune their oscillators.

4. EOX: Used as a flag to indicate the end of a System Exclusive transmission (see Table VI).

TABLE V
SYSTEM REAL TIME MESSAGES

STATUS	DATA BYTES	DESCRIPTION
11111000		Timing Clock
11111001		Undefined
11111010		Start
11111011		Continue
11111100		Stop
11111101		Undefined
11111110		Active Sensing
11111111		System Reset

NOTES:

1. The System Real Time messages are for synchronizing all of the system in real time.

2. The Sytem Real Time messages can be sent at any time. Any messages that consist of two or more bytes may be split to insert Real Time messages.

3. Timing Clock (F8H)
The system is synchronized with this clock, which is sent at a rate of 24 clocks/quarter note.

4. Start (from the beginning of song) (FAH)
This byte is immediately sent when the PLAY switch on the master (e.g. sequencer or rhythm unit) is pressed.

5. Continue (FBH)
This is sent when the CONTINUE switch is hit. A sequence will continue at the time of the next clock.

6. Stop (FCH)
This byte is immediately sent when the STOP switch is hit. It will stop the sequence.

7. Active Sensing (FEH)
Use of this message is optional, for either receivers or transmitters. This is a "dummy" Status byte that is sent every 300 ms (max), whenever there is no other activity on MIDI. The receiver will operate normally if it never receives FEH. Otherwise, if FEH is ever received, the receiver will expect to receive FEH or a transmission of any type every 300 ms (max). If a period of 300 ms passes with no activity, the receiver will turn off the voices and return to normal operation.

8. System Reset (FFH)
This message initializes all of the system to the condition of just having turned on power. The System Reset message should be used sparingly, preferably under manual command only. In particular, it should not be sent automatically on power-up.

TABLE VI
SYSTEM EXCLUSIVE MESSAGES

STATUS	DATA BYTES	DESCRIPTION
11110000		Bulk dump etc.
	0iiiiiii	iiiiiii:identification
	•	
	(0*******)	
		Any number of bytes
	•	may be sent here,
		for any purpose, as
	•	long as they all
		have a zero in the
	•	most significant
		bit.
	(0*******)	
	•	
	11110111	EOX: "End of System Exclusive"

NOTES:
1. iiiiiii: identification ID (0-127)

2. All bytes between the System Exclusive Status byte and EOX or the next Status byte must have zeros in the MSB.

3. The ID number can be obtained from the MIDI committee.

4. In no case should other Status or Data bytes (except Real-Time) be interleaved with System Exclusive, regardless of whether or not the ID code is recognized.

5. EOX or any other Status byte, except Real-Time, will terminate a System Exclusive message, and should be sent immediately at its conclusion.

MIDI 1.0 Specification Updates

Permanent Manufacturer ID Codes
(as of September 1986)

ID Number	*Manufacturer*
01H	Sequential
03H	Octave Plateau
04H	Moog
05H	Passport Designs
06H	Lexicon
07H	Kurzweil
08H	Fender
0FH	Ensoniq
10H	Oberheim
15H	J L Cooper
16H	Lowrey
18H	E-mu Systems
19H	Harmony Systems
1AH	ART
1BH	Baldwin
21H	SIEL
22H	Synthaxe
24H	Hohner
26H	Solton
27H	Jellinghaus Musik Systeme
29H	PPG
2FH	Elka
40H	Kawai
41H	Roland
42H	Korg
43H	Yamaha
44H	Casio
46H	Kamiya Studio
47H	Akai
48H	Japan Victor
49H	Meisoshsa

Temporary Manufacturer ID Codes
(as of September 1986)

ID Number	Manufacturer	Temp Expires
02H	IDP	6/02/87
09H	Data Stream Inc.	6/02/87
0AH	AKG Acoustics	6/02/87
0BH	Voyce Music	6/02/87
0DH	ADA Signal Proc	6/02/87
0EH	Garfield Electronics	6/02/87
1CH	Eventide	2/10/87
11H	Apple Computer	6/02/87
13H	Mimetics	6/26/86
1DH	Inventronics	4/04/87
1EH	Key Concept	4/10/87
1FH	Clarity	4/11/87
28H	CTM	8/01/87
2AH	JEN	10/26/86
2BH	SSL Limited	1/21/87
2CH	Audio Vertriebel-Peter Struven Gmbh	4/10/87
2EH	Soundtracs Ltd.	5/08/87
30H	Dynacord	6/02/87
45H	Moridaira	12/20/86
4AH	Hoshino Gakki	12/19/86
4BH	Fujitsu Electronics	9/28/87

Any manufacturer may request a System Exclusive ID code. Temporary ID numbers are granted for one year by the MMA. If the manufacturer uses that number in a product and publicly publishes the format used within the year, the number becomes permanent. Contact the MMA for full details.

14-BIT CONTROLLERS (MSB'S)

Decimal	Definition	Hex
0	undefined	00H
1	Modulation Controller	01H
2	Breath Controller	02H
3	undefined	03H
4	Foot Controller	04H
5	Portamento Time	05H
6	Data Entry MSB	06H
7	Main Volume	07H
8	Balance Controller	08H
9	undefined	09H
10	Pan Controller	0AH
11	Expression Controller	0BH
12	undefined	0CH
13	undefined	0DH
14	undefined	0EH
15	undefined	0FH
16	General Purpose Controller #1	10H
17	General Purpose Controller #2	11H
18	General Purpose Controller #3	12H
19	General Purpose Controller #4	13H
20	undefined	14H
|	undefined	|
31	undefined	1FH

14-BIT CONTROLLERS (LSB'S)

Decimal	Definition	Hex
32	LSB for Controller 0	20H
|	LSB for Controllers 1-30	|
63	LSB for Controller 31	3FH

7-BIT CONTROLLERS

Decimal	Definition	Hex
64	Hold, Damper Pedal (sustain)	40H
65	Portamento	41H
66	Sostenuto	42H
67	Soft Pedal	43H
68	undefined	44H
69	Hold 2	45H
70	undefined	46H
|	undefined	|
79	undefined	4FH
80	General Purpose Controller #5	50H
81	General Purpose Controller #6	51H
82	General Purpose Controller #7	52H
83	General Purpose Controller #8	53H
84	undefined	54H
|	undefined	|
91	undefined	5BH
92	Tremolo Depth	5CH
93	Chorus Depth	5DH
94	Detune (Celeste)	5EH
95	Phaser Depth	5FH

PARAMETER VALUE

Decimal	Definition	Hex
96	Data Increment	60H
97	Data Decrement	61H

PARAMETER SELECTION

Decimal	Definition	Hex
98	Non-Registered Parameter LSB	62H
99	Non-Registered Parameter MSB	63H
100	Registered Parameter Number LSB	64H
101	Registered Parameter Number MSB	65H

UNDEFINED CONTROLLERS

Decimal	Definition	Hex
102	undefined	66H
|	undefined	|
121	undefined	79H

RESERVED FOR CHANNEL MODE MESSAGES

Decimal	Definition	Hex
122	LOCAL CONTROL ON/OFF	7AH
123	ALL NOTES OFF	7BH
124	OMNI MODE OFF (ALL NOTES OFF)	7CH
125	OMNI MODE ON (ALL NOTES OFF)	7DH
126	MONO MODE ON (ALL NOTES OFF)	7EH
127	POLY MODE ON (ALL NOTES OFF)	7FH

NOTES:

• *Continuous Switches* : The JMSC and MMA have agreed to alter the definitions of Controllers 64-95 (40-5FH) from switches to continuous controllers with 7-bit resolution. When used as ON/OFF switches, the following convention should be used on all current implementations:

OFF = 0-63 (00-3FH)
ON = 64-127 (40-7FH)

This differs from the two conventions used in earlier implementations.

[1] This is the convention defined in the original specification:

OFF = 0 (00H)
ON = 127 (7FH)
(values 1-126 (01-7EH) inclusive are ignored)

[2] This convention was also used in some earlier implementations:

OFF = 0 (00H)
ON = 1-127 (01-7F)

Some incompatibility problems may occur between instruments with old and current implementations. Data values of 0 and 127 (00H and 7FH) will always be recognized as OFF and ON respectively. Intermediate data values might not be transmitted or recognized as the same switch state on devices with differerent implementations, since there are three possible data ranges for OFF and ON.

Comparison Of Switch Controller
On / Off Data Ranges

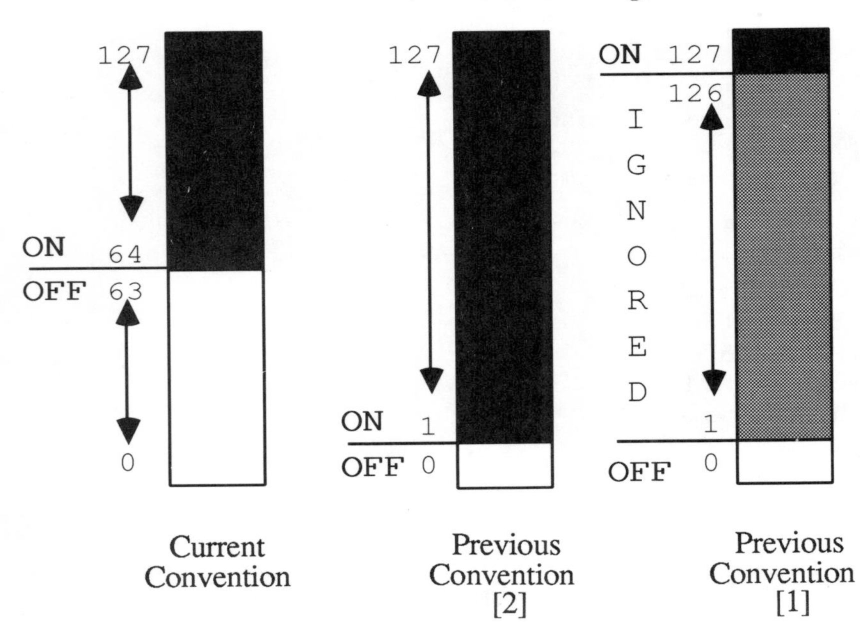

Current Convention

Previous Convention [2]

Previous Convention [1]

• *Global Controllers* : In Mode 4, a controller that should affect all assigned voices equally should be transmitted on a channel number equal to the Basic Channel minus one. For example, if the receiver's assigned basic channel is 4, global controller messages should be transmitted on channel 3. If the receiver's assigned basic channel is 1, then global controller messages should be transmitted on channel 16.

- To afford greater control flexibility within a MIDI system, all sound parameters of an instrument should be accessible via Registered or Non-Registered Numbers.

- Manufacturers may assign any parameter to any Non-Registered Parameter Number. A list of assignments should be published in the owner's manual.

- The value of Registered or Non-Registered Parameters are altered by Data Entry MSB (06H), Data Entry LSB (26H), Data Increment (60H), or Data Decrement (61H) control change messages as follows: First transmit the Registered or Non-Registered Parameter Number corresponding to the parameter to be accessed, then transmit the desired Data Entry, Data Increment, or Data Decrement value for the parameter.

- Once the reception of Non-Registered and/or Registered Parameter Numbers has been enabled, the receiver should wait until it receives both an LSB and MSB for a Parameter Number, to verify it is operating on the correct parameter.

- The transmitter may send only an LSB or only an MSB to change the Parameter Number, and the receiver should be able to respond accordingly. However, since the transmitter has no idea when the reception was enabled on the receiver, and since the receiver is waiting (at least initially) for both the LSB and the MSB, it is suggested that the transmitter send out the LSB and MSB each time a new parameter number is selected.

- Once a new Parameter Number is chosen, it retains its old value until a new Data Entry, Data Increment, or Data Decrement is received.

- Registered Parameter Numbers are defined jointly by the MMA and JMSC. Since this is a standardized list, reception of Registered Parameter Numbers may be enabled at power-up. All other rules for their use are the same as those for Non-Registered Parameters.

- At this time the only defined Registered Parameter Number is 00, **Pitch Bend Sensitivity**. The MSB of the data is in semitone resolution, and the LSB of the data is in units of 1/128th of a semitone. For example, value of MSB=02H, LSB =20H means +/- 2.25 semitones (total range of 4.50 semitones).

All System Exclusive messages must conform to this basic shell:

<SysEx> (F0H)
<ID Code>
<data bytes>
<EOX> (F7H)

At this time, there are four defined ID codes:
1. Manufacturer (see *Specification Updates* for a complete list)
2. Universal Non-Commercial (7DH)
3. Universal Non-Real Time (7EH)
4. Universal Real Time (7FH)

SYSTEM EXCLUSIVE FORMATS:

Each ID code is associated with a particular extension of the basic System Exclusive format shell.

• ***Manufacturer System Exclusive Messages***
<SysEx>
<ID: Manufacturer>
<data bytes>
<EOX>
Only the basic shell is defined. Specific formats are designed and published by the manufacturer.

• ***Universal Non-Commercial System Exclusive Messages***
<SysEx>
< ID: Universal Non-Commercial>
<data bytes>
<EOX>
Only the basic shell is defined.

• ***Universal Non-Real Time System Exclusive Messages***
<SysEx>
< ID: Universal Non-Real Time>
<Device Channel>
<Sub-ID1>
<Sub-ID2>
<data bytes>
<EOX>

This is the basic shell for all Universal Non-Real Time System Exclusive Messages. The Device Channel Data byte specifies which unit within the system the message is intended for. Legal values for the Device Channel are 0-127 (00-7FH). A device channel value of 127 (7FH) indicates the message is intended for all units in the system. The Sub -ID Data bytes are used to identify the specific message. There are currently eight defined Sub-ID's:

Sample Dump Header	=	1 (01H)
Sample Dump Data Packet	=	2 (02H)
Dump Request	=	3 (03H)
MIDI Time Code Set-up	=	4 (04H)
WAIT	=	124 (7CH)
CANCEL	=	125 (7DH)
NAK	=	126 (7EH)
ACK	=	127 (7FH)

(Detailed information about the messages specified by the Sub-ID's is given in *Sample Dump Standard, MIDI Time Code Specification,* and *MIDI At A Glance.*)

NOTE: The Non-Real Time messages defined by the Sample Dump Standard and MIDI Time Code Specification were adopted before the format for Universal Non-Real Time Messages was finalized. Although some contain only one Sub-ID, they are considered to be legal Non-Real Time messages.

• ***Universal Real Time System Exclusive Messages***

<SysEx>
<ID: Universal Real Time>
<Device Channel>
<Sub ID1>
<Sub ID2>
<data bytes>
<EOX>

This is the basic shell for all Universal Real Time System Exclusive Messages. The Device Channel Data byte specifies which unit within the system the message is intended for. Legal values for the Device Channel are 0-127 (00-7FH). A device channel value of 127 (7FH) indicates the message is intended for all units in the system. The Sub -ID Data bytes are used to identify the specific message. Currently defined Sub-ID's are:

Sub ID1:
Long Form Time Code ID = 1 (01H)

Sub ID2:
Full Time Code Message = 0(00H)
User Bits Message = 1(01H)

(Detailed information about the messages specified by the Sub-ID's is given in *MIDI Time Code Specification* and *MIDI At A Glance.*)

1.0 SAMPLE DUMP DATA FORMAT

1.1 **DUMP HEADER**

<SysEx>
<ID: Universal Non-Real Time>
<Channel Number>
<Sub ID:Header>
<Sample Number> (2 bytes, LSB first)
<Sample Format>
<Sample Period> (3 bytes, LSB first)
<Sample Length> (3 bytes, LSB first)
<Sustain Loop Start Point> (3 bytes, LSB first)
<Sustair. Loop End Point> (3 bytes, LSB first)
<Loop Type>
<EOX>

1.2 **DATA PACKET**

<SysEx>
<ID: Universal Non-Real Time>
<Channel Number>
<Sub ID: Data Packet>
<Packet Number>
<Sample Data> (120 data bytes)
<Checksum>
<EOX>

2.0 SAMPLE DUMP MESSAGES

2.1 **DUMP REQUEST**: "Please send sample"

<SysEx>
<ID: Universal Non-Real Time>
<Channel Number>
<Sub ID: Dump Request>
<Sample Number> (2 bytes, LSB first)
<EOX>

2.2 **Handshaking Flags**

2.2.1 **ACK:** "Last packet received correctly, start sending the next one."

<SysEx>
<ID: Universal Non-Real Time>
<Channel Number>
<Sub ID: ACK>
<Packet Number>
<EOX>

2.2.2 **NAK:** "Last packet not received correctly, please resend."

<SysEx>
<ID: Universal Non-Real Time>
<Channel Number>
<Sub ID: NAK>
<Packet Number>
<EOX>

2.2.3 **CANCEL**: "Abort dump."

<SysEx>

<ID: Universal Non-Real Time>
<Channel Number>
<Sub ID: CANCEL>
<Packet Number>

<EOX>

2.2.4 **WAIT:** "Pause dump indefinitely until next message is received."

<SysEx>

<ID: Universal Non-Real Time>
<Channel Number>
<Sub ID: WAIT>
<Packet Number>

<EOX>

*MIDI Sample Dump Standard**

This standard is used for dumping sample data between MIDI devices (samplers, computers, etc.) It is designed to work as an open or closed loop system, with handshaking in the closed loop to aid speed and provide error recovery. Handshaking also accommodates machines that may need more time to process incoming data. The open loop system may be used by those who wish to implement a simplified version without handshaking.

The basic messages are DUMP REQUEST, ACK, NAK, CANCEL, WAIT, DUMP HEADER, and DATA PACKET. (In theory, the 4 handshaking flags (ACK/NAK/CANCEL/WAIT) may be used for other Universal Non-Real Time System Exclusive messages and communications.)

Desciptions of each message are given below, followed by a description of the dump procedure. (Values given in the message descriptions are hexadecimal.)

SAMPLE DUMP DATA FORMATS

DUMP HEADER

F0 7E cc 01 ss ss ee ff ff ff gg gg gg hh hh hh ii ii ii jj F7

cc = channel number
ss ss = sample number (LSB first)
ee = sample format (# significant bits, from 8-28)
ff ff ff = sample period (1/sample rate), in nanoseconds (LSB first)
gg gg gg = sample length, in words (LSB first)
hh hh hh = sustain loop start point (word number) (LSB first)
ii ii ii = sustain loop end point (word number) (LSB first)
jj = loop type (00=forwards only; 01=backwards/forwards)

DATA PACKET

F0 7E cc 02 kk <120 bytes> ll F7

cc = channel number
kk = running packet count (00-7F)
ll = checksum (XOR of 7E, cc, 02, kk, <120 bytes>)

The total size of a data packet is 127 bytes. This is to avoid overflow of MIDI input buffers in machines that may want to receive an entire message before processing it. (128 bytes, or a 1/2 page of memory, is considered the smallest reasonable buffer for current MIDI devices.)

A data packet consists of its own header, a packet number, 120 bytes of data, a checksum, and an End Of Exclusive message (EOX). The packet number begins at 00 and increments with each new packet. It resets to 00 after it reaches 7F. This packet number is used by the receiver to distinguish between a new data packet, or a resend of a previous data packet. The packet number is followed by 120 bytes of data, which form 60, 40, or 30 words (MSB first).

The number of words formed by the 120 data bytes is determined by the sample format. Each data byte holds 7 bits. If the sample format is 8-14 bits, 2 bytes form a word (60 words/packet), 15-21 bits require 3 bytes/word (40 words/packet), and 22-28 bits require 4 bytes/word (30 words/packet). Information is left-justified within the 7-bit bytes, and unused bits will be filled with zeroes.

*NOTE: The standard for dumping sample data evolved as a series of proposals submitted jointly to the JMSC and MMA. The final version of the proposal was adopted in January 1986 by the JMSC and MMA. The adopted proposal presented the Sample Dump Standard in the context of a firmware implementation for a specific instrument. In the interest of presenting the Sample Dump Standard clearly and unambiguously, we have removed device specific information, references to previous proposals, and information not relevant to the adopted standard. To this same end, we have also added headings and re-organized the material (very slightly) in order to keep relevant topics together. This is an accurate and complete description of the adopted standard.

For example, a sample word of FFFH will be sent as 01111111B 01111100B (FFFH represents a full positive value and 000H represents full negative). The checksum is the XOR of 7E, <channel>, 02, <packet number>, and the 120 data bytes.

SAMPLE DUMP MESSAGES

DUMP REQUEST

F0 7E cc 03 ss ss F7
cc = channel number
ss ss = sample number (the requested sample), LSB first

Upon receiving this message, the sampler checks the sample number (ss ss) to see if it is within legal range. If it is, the requested sample is dumped to the requesting device following the procedures outlined below. If it is not within range, the message is ignored.

Handshaking Messages

Packet numbers are included in the handshaking commands to accommodate future machines that might have the intelligence to re-transmit specific packets after the entire dump is finished or if synchronization is lost.

ACK

F0 7E cc 7F pp F7
cc = channel number
pp = packet number

This handshaking flag means "Last packet received correctly, start sending the next one." The packet number reflects which packet is being acknowledged as correct.

NAK

F0 7E cc 7E pp F7
cc = channel number
pp = packet number

This handshaking flag means "Last data packet not received correctly, please resend." The packet number reflects which packet is being rejected.

CANCEL

F0 7E cc 7D pp F7
cc = channel number
pp = packet

This handshaking flag means "Abort dump." The packet number reflects the packet on which the abort occurs.

WAIT

F0 7E cc 7C pp F7
cc = channel number
pp = packet number

This handsaking flag means "Pause the dump indefinitely, until the next message is received." It is used when unit receiving the dump (terminal support computer, etc.) needs to perform other functions (disk access, for example) before receiving the remainder of the dump. The next message received will determine if the dump continues or aborts.

*DUMP PROCEDURE : MASTER (SOURCE OF SAMPLE DATA)**

Once a dump has been requested either via MIDI or from the front panel, the DUMP HEADER is sent. After sending the header, the master must time out for at least two seconds, allowing the receiver to decide if it will accept this sample (enough memory, etc.).

If it receives a CANCEL within this time, it should abort the dump immediately (reception of any illegal message may also abort the dump). If it receives an ACK, it will start sending data packets immediately. If it receives a WAIT, it pauses indefinitely until another message is received (it then processes the message as it normally would). If nothing is received within the timeout, the master assumes an open loop system, and sends the first packet.

After sending each packet, a device should time out for at least 20 milliseconds and watch its MIDI In port. If an ACK is received, it sends the next packet immediately. It receives a NAK, and the packet number matches the previous packet number, the previous packet is resent. If the packet numbers don't match, and the device isn't capable of sending packets out of order, the NAK is ignored.

If a WAIT is received, a device should watch its MIDI In port indefinitely for another message. When the message is received it should be processed like a normal ACK, NAK, CANCEL, or illegal message. (By using the WAIT command, the slave can pause a sampler in the middle of a dump while it saves part of the sample to disk, etc.)

If no messages are received within the 20 milliseconds following the transmission of a data packet, the device may assume an open loop system and send the next packet.

This process continues until there are less than 121 bytes to send. The final packet will still consist of 120 bytes, regardless of how many significant bytes actually remain, and the unused bytes will be filled with zeroes. The device receiving the dump should handshake after receiving the last packet.

DUMP PROCEDURE: SLAVE (DESTINATION OF SAMPLE DATA)

When receiving a sample dump, a device should keep a running checksum during reception. If the checksum matches the checksum in the data packet, it will send an ACK and wait for the next packet. If they do not match, it will send a NAK containing the packet number of the packet that caused the checksum error. It then waits for the next packet. If, after sending the NAK, the packet number of the next packet doesn't match the previous packet number, and the unit is not capable of accepting packets out of order, the error is ignored and the dump continues as if the checksums had matched.

If the receiving device runs out of memory before the dump is completed, it should transmit a CANCEL to the master to stop the dump.

***NOTE: An operational flowchart and communication protocols for the sample dump procedures described below are contained in the *Inside MIDI* section of this book.**

1.0 TIME CODE MESSAGES

1.1 QUARTER FRAME MESSAGE BASIC FORMAT

<SysCom: QUARTER FRAME>
<Type/Data>

The first byte of the message is the Quarter Frame System Common Status byte (F1H). The second byte of the message is split into two bit fields:
0nnn dddd.

nnn defines the Quarter Frame message *type* and **dddd** is a 4-bit nibble of binary *data* for the specified message type. Examples of each type and data format are given below.

These messages should be thought of as groups of eight, since it takes eight different Quarter Frame messages to specify a complete SMPTE time. They are listed here in the order they are transmitted when time code is running forward. The reverse order is used when time code is running backward.

1.1.1 **QUARTER FRAME: Type = 0**
<SysCom: QUARTER FRAME>
<Frame Count LS Nibble/Data>

1.1.2 **QUARTER FRAME: Type = 1**
<SysCom: QUARTER FRAME>
<Frame Count MS Nibble/Data>

The LS and MS nibbles of the frame count are assembled as follows:
Frame Count: xxx yyyyy
xxx = undefined and reserved
yyyyy = Frame Number (0-29)

1.1.3 **QUARTER FRAME: Type = 2**
<SysCom: QUARTER FRAME>
<Seconds Count LS Nibble/Data>

1.1.4 **QUARTER FRAME: Type = 3**
<SysCom: QUARTER FRAME>
<Seconds Count MS Nibble/Data>

The LS and MS nibbles of the second count are assembled as follows:
Seconds Count: xx yyyyyy
xx = undefined and reserved
yyyyyy = Seconds Count (0-59)

1.1.5 **QUARTER FRAME: Type = 4**
<SysCom: QUARTER FRAME>
<Minutes Count LS Nibble/Data>

1.1.6 **QUARTER FRAME: Type = 5**
<SysCom: QUARTER FRAME>
<Minutes Count MS Nibble/Data>

The LS and MS nibbles of the minute count are assembled as follows:
Minutes Count: xx yyyyyy
xx = undefined and reserved
yyyyyy = Minutes Count (0-59)

1.1.7 **QUARTER FRAME: Type = 6**

<SysCom: QUARTER FRAME>

<Hours Count LS Nibble/Data>

1.1.8 **QUARTER FRAME: Type = 7**

<SysCom: QUARTER FRAME>

<Hours Count MS Nibble/SMPTE Type/Data>

The LS and MS nibbles of the hour count are assembled as follows:

Hours Count: x yy zzzzz

x = undefined and reserved

yy = Time Code Type:

0 = 24 Frames/Second

1 = 25 Frames/Second

2 = 30 Frames/Second (drop frame)

3 = 30 Frames/Second (non-drop frame)

zzzzz = Hours Count (0-23)

1.2 FULL MESSAGE

<SysEx>

<ID: Universal Real Time>

<Channel Number: All devices>

<Sub-ID1: Long Form Time Code>

<Sub-ID2: Full Time Code Message>

<Hours/Type>

<Minutes>

<Seconds>

<Frames>

<EOX>

1.3 USER BITS MESSAGE

<SysEx>

<ID: Universal Real Time>

<Channel Number: All devices>

<Sub-ID1: Long Form Time Code>

<Sub-ID2: User Bits Messages>

<User Bits> (8 bytes, data in LS 4 bits only)

<Format Code> (1 byte, data in LS 2 bits only)

<EOX>

2.0 SET-UP MESSAGES

2.1 BASIC FORMAT

<SysEx>

<ID: Universal Non-Real Time>

<Channel Number>

<Sub-ID 1: Time Code Set-Up>

<Sub ID 2: Set-Up Type>

<Hours/Type>

<Minutes>

<Seconds>

<Frames>

<Fractional Frames>

<Event Number or Special Type> (2 bytes, LSB first)

<additional info> (optional data sent as nibbles, LS nibble first)

<EOX>

2.2 SET-UP TYPES

00 = Special
01 = Punch In Points
02 = Punch Out Points
03 = Delete Punch In Point
04 = Delete Punch Out Point
05 = Event Start Points
06 = Event Stop Point
07 = Event Start Points with additional info
08 = Event Stop Points with additional info
09 = Delete Event Start Point
0A = Delete Event Stop Point
0B = Cue Points
0C = Cue Points with additional info
0D = Delete Cue Point
0E = Event Name in additional info

2.3 SPECIAL TYPES

00 00 = Time Code Offset
01 00 = Enable Event List
02 00 = Disable Event List
03 00 = Clear Event List
04 00 = System Stop

MIDI Time Code Detailed Specification

(Supplement to MIDI 1.0)

Chris Meyer
Evan Books
28 October 1986

JUSTIFICATION FOR MIDI TIME CODE

The merit of implementing the MIDI Time Code proposal within the current MIDI specification is as follows:

SMPTE has become the *de facto* timing reference standard in the professional audio world and in almost the entire video world. SMPTE is also seeing more and more use in the semi-professional audio area. We hope to combine this universal timing reference, SMPTE, with the *de facto* standard for controlling musical equipment, MIDI.

Encoding SMPTE over MIDI allows a person to work with one timing reference throughout the entire system. For example, studio engineers are more familiar with the idea of telling a multitrack recorder to punch in and out of record mode at specific SMPTE times, as opposed to a specific beat in a specific bar. To force a musician or studio engineer to convert back and forth between a SMPTE time and a specific bar number is tedious and should not be necessary (one would have to take into account tempo and tempo changes, etc.).

Also, some operations are referenced only as SMPTE times, as opposed to beats in a bar. For example, creating audio and sound effects for video requires that certain sounds and sequences be played at specific SMPTE times. There is no other easy way to do this with Song Position Pointers, etc., and even if there was, it would be an unnatural way for a video or recording engineer to work.

MIDI Time Code is an absolute timing reference, whereas MIDI Clock and Song Position Pointer are relative timing references. In virtually all audio for film/video work, SMPTE is already being used as the main time base, and any musical passages which need to be recorded are usually done by getting a MIDI-based sequencer to start at a pre-determined SMPTE time code. In most cases, though, it is SMPTE which is the Master timing reference being used. In order for MIDI-based devices to operate on an absolute time code which is independent of tempo, MIDI Time Code must be used. Existing devices merely translate SMPTE into MIDI Clocks and Song Position Pointers based upon a given tempo. This is not absolute time, but relative time and all of the SMPTE cue points will change if the tempo changes. The majority of sound effects work for film and video does not involve musical passages with tempos, rather it involves individual sound effect "events" which must occur at specific, absolute times, not relative to any "tempo".

MIDI TIME CODE SYSTEM COMPONENTS

SMPTE TO MTC CONVERTER

This box would either convert longitudinal (audio-type) or vertical (video-type) SMPTE time code from a master timing device into MTC. The function could be integrated into video tape recorders (VTRs) or synchronization units that control audio tape recorders (ATRs). Alternately, a stand-alone box would do the conversion, or simply generate MTC directly. Note that conversion from MTC to SMPTE time code is not envisioned, as it is of little practical value.

CUE LIST MANAGER

This would be a device or computer program that would maintain a cue list of desired events, and send the list to the slaves. For performance, the manager might pass the Time Code from the SMPTE-MTC converter through to the slaves, or, in a stand-alone system it might generate Time Code itself. This "central controller" would presumably also contain all library functions for downloading sound programs, samples, sequences, patterns, and so on, to the slaves. A Cue List Manager would pre-load intelligent MTC peripherals (see below) with this data.

MTC SEQUENCER

To control existing equipment or any device which does not recognize MTC in an MTC system, this device would be needed. It would receive the cue list from the manager and convert the cues into normal MIDI commands. At the specified SMPTE times, the sequencer would then send the MIDI commands to the specific devices. For example, for existing MIDI equipment it might provide MIDI messages such as Note On, Note Off, Song Select, Start, Stop, Program Changes, etc. Non-MIDI equipment (such as CD players, mixing consoles, lighting, sound effects cartridge units and ATRs) may also be controlled if such a device had relay controls.

INTELLIGENT MTC PERIPHERAL

In this category belong devices capable of receiving an MTC Cue List from the manager, and triggering themselves appropriately when the correct Time Code (SMPTE or MIDI) has been received. Above this minimum, the device might be able to change its programming in response to the Cue List, or prepare itself for ensuing events.

For example, an intelligent MTC-equipped analog multitrack tape machine might read in a list of punch in/punch out cues from the Cue List Manager, and then alter them to internally compensate for its bias current rise and fall times. A sampling-based sound effects device might preload samples from its own disk drive into a RAM buffer, in anticipation of needing them for cues later on in the cue list.

It should be mentioned that, while these functions are separately described, actual devices may incorporate a mixture of these functions, suited to specific applications in their market.

A MIDI TIME CODE SYSTEM

The MIDI Time Code format contains two parts: Time Code and Set-Up. Time Code is relatively straightforward: hours, minutes, seconds, and frame numbers (approximately 1/30 of a second) are encoded and distributed throughout the MIDI system so that all the units know exactly what time it is.

Set-Up, however, is where MTC gains its power. It is a format for informing MIDI devices of events to be performed at specific times. Ultimately, this aspect of MTC will lead to the creation of an entirely new class of production equipment. Before getting into the nuts and bolts of the spec itself, let's talk about some of the uses and features of forthcoming devices that have been envisioned.

Set-up begins with the concept of a cue list. In video editing, for example, it is customary to transfer the video master source tapes, which may be on expensive, two-inch recorders, to less-expensive recorders. The editing team then works over this copy, making a list of all the segments that they want to piece together as they are defined by their SMPTE times.

For example, the first scene starts at time A and ends at time B, the next scene starts at time C and ends at time D. A third scene may even lie between the first two. When done, they feed this cue list time information into the editing system of the master recorder(s) or just give the cue list to an editor who does the work manually. The editing system or editor then locates the desired segments and assembles them in the proper sequence.

Now suppose that, instead of one or two video recorders, we have twenty devices that will play a part in our audio/video or film production: special effects generators for fades and superimpositions, additional decks with background scenery, live cameras, MIDI sequencers, drum machines, synthesizers, samplers, DDLs, soundtrack decks, CDs, effects devices, and so on. As it stands now, each of these devices must be handled more or less separately, with painstaking and time-consuming assembly editing or multitrack overdubs. And when a change in the program occurs (which always happens), anywhere from just a few items to the whole system may need to be reprogrammed by hand.

This is where MIDI Time Code comes in. It can potentially control all of these individual production elements so that they function together from a single cue list. The master controller which would handle this function is described as a Cue List Manager. On such a console, you would list what you want each device to do, and when to do it. The manager would then send the cue list to the various machines via the MTC Set-Up protocol. Each unit would then react as programmed when the designated MIDI Time Code (or conventional SMPTE Time Code) appears. Changes? No problem. Simply edit the cue list using simple word-processing functions, then run the tape again.

MTC thus integrates into a manageable system all of the diverse tools at our disposal. It would drastically reduce the time, money, and frustration needed to produce a film or video.

Having covered the basic aspects of a MIDI Time Code system, as well as examples of how an overall system might function, we will now take a look at the actual MIDI specification itself.

TIME CODE MESSAGES

For device synchronization, Time Code uses two basic types of messages, described as Quarter Frame and Full. There is also a third, optional message for encoding SMPTE user bits.

QUARTER FRAME MESSAGES

Quarter Frame messages are used only while the system is running. They are rather like the PPQN or MIDI clocks to which we are accustomed. But there are several important ways in which Quarter Frame messages differ from the other systems.

As their name implies, they have fine resolution. If we assume 30 frames per second, there will be 120 Quarter Frame messages per second. This corresponds to a maximum latency of 8.3 milliseconds (at 30 frames per second), with accuracy greater than this possible within the specific device (which may interpolate in between quarter frames to "bit" resolution). Quarter Frame messages serve a dual purpose: besides providing the basic timing pulse for the system, each message contains a unique nibble (four bits) defining a digit of a specific field of the current SMPTE time.

Quarter frame messages should be thought of as groups of eight messages. One of these groups encodes the SMPTE time in hours, minutes, seconds, and frames. Since it takes eight quarter frames for a complete time code message, the complete SMPTE time is updated every two frames. Each quarter frame message contains two bytes. The first byte is F1, the Quarter Frame System Common byte. The second byte contains a nibble that represents the message number (0 through 7), and a nibble for one of the digits of a time field (hours, minutes, seconds, or frames).

QUARTER FRAME MESSAGES (2 BYTES):

F1 <message>

F1 = Currently unused and undefined System Common status
byte <message> = 0nnn dddd

dddd = 4 bits of binary data for this Message Type
nnn = Message Type:
- 0 = Frame count LS nibble
- 1 = Frame count MS nibble
- 2 = Seconds count LS nibble
- 3 = Seconds count MS nibble
- 4 = Minutes count LS nibble
- 5 = Minutes count MS nibble
- 6 = Hours count LS nibble
- 7 = Hours count MS nibble and SMPTE Type

After both the MS nibble and the LS nibble of the above counts are assembled, their bit fields are assigned as follows:

FRAME COUNT:

xxx = undefined and reserved for future use.
Transmitter must set these bits to 0 and receiver should ignore!

yyyyy = Frame number (0-29)

SECONDS COUNT:

xx yyyyyy

xx = undefined and reserved for future use. Transmitter must set these bits to 0 and receiver should ignore!
yyyyyy = Seconds Count (0-59)

MINUTES COUNT:

xx yyyyyy

xx = undefined and reserved for future use. Transmitter must set these bits to 0 and receiver should ignore!
yyyyyy = Minutes Count (0-59)

HOURS COUNT;

xyy zzzzz

x = undefined and reserved for future use. Transmitter must set this bit to 0 and receiver should ignore!

yy = Time Code Type:
- 0 = 24 Frames/Second
- 1 = 25 Frames/Second
- 2 = 30 Frames/Second (Drop-Frame)
- 3 = 30 Frames/Second (Non-Drop)

zzzzz = Hours Count (0-23)

QUARTER FRAME MESSAGE IMPLEMENTATION

When time code is running in the forward direction, the device producing the MIDI Time Code will send Quarter Frame messages at quarter frame intervals in the following order:

F1 0X
F1 1X
F1 2X
F1 3X
F1 4X
F1 5X
F1 6X
F1 7X

after which the sequence repeats itself, at a rate of one complete 8-message sequence every 2 frames (8 quarter frames). When time code is running in reverse, the quarter frame messages are sent in reverse order, starting with F1 7X and ending with F1 0X. Again, at least 8 quarter frame messages must be sent. The arrival of the F1 0X and F1 4X messages always denote frame boundaries.

Since 8 quarter frame messages are required to definitely establish the actual SMPTE time, timing lock cannot be achieved until the reader has read a full sequence of 8 messages, from first message to last. This will take from 2 to 4 frames to do, depending on when the reader comes on line.

During fast forward, rewind, or shuttle modes, the time code generator should stop sending quarter frame messages, and just send a Full Message once the final destination has been reached. The generator can then pause for any devices to shuttle to that point, and resume by sending quarter frame messages when play mode is resumed. The time code indicated in the Full Message takes effect upon receipt of the first quarter frame message after the Full Message.

Do not send quarter frame messages continuously in a shuttle mode at high speed, since this unnecessarily clogs the MIDI data lines. If you must periodically update a device's time code during a long shuttle, then send a Full Message every so often.

The quarter frame message F1 0X (Frame Count LS nibble) must be sent on a frame boundary. The frame number indicated by the frame count is the number of the frame which starts on that boundary. This follows the same convention as normal SMPTE longitudinal time code, where bit 00 of the 80-bit message arrives at the precise time that the frame it represents is actually starting. The SMPTE time will be incremented by 2 frames for each 8-message sequence, since an 8-message sequence will take 2 frames to send. For closest timing, it is suggested that this message be pre-released by the transmitter so that the last bit of the 2nd byte arrives at the frame boundary.

Another way to look at it is: When the last quarter frame message (F1 7X) arrives and the time can be fully assembled, the information is now actually 2 frames old. A receiver of this time must keep an internal offset of +2 frames for displaying. This may seem unusual, but it is the way normal SMPTE is received and also makes backing up (running time code backwards) less confusing — when receiving the 8 quarter frame messages backwards, the F1 0X message still falls on the boundary of the frame it represents.

Each quarter frame message number (0—>7) indicates which of the 8 quarter frames of the 2-frame sequence we are on. For example, message 0 (F1 0X) indicates quarter frame 1 of frame #1 in the sequence, and message 4 (F1 4X) indicates quarter frame 1 of frame #2 in the sequence. If a reader receives these message numbers in descending sequence, then it knows that time code is being sent in the reverse direction. Also, a reader can come on line at any time and know exactly where it is in relation to the 2-frame sequence, down to a quarter frame accuracy.

It is the responsibility of the time code reader to ensure that MTC is being properly interpreted. This requires waiting a sufficient amount of time in order to achieve time code lock, and maintaining that lock until synchronization is dropped. Although each passing quarter frame message could be interpreted as a relative quarter frame count, the time code reader should always verify the actual complete time code after every 8-message sequence (2 frames) in order to guarantee a proper lock.

For example, let's assume the time is 01:37:52:16 (30 frames per second, non-drop). Since the time is sent from least to most significant digit, the first two Quarter Frame messages will contain the data 16 (frames), the second two will contain the data 52 (seconds), the third two will represent 37 (minutes), and the final two encode the 1 (hours and SMPTE Type). The Quarter Frame Messages description defines how the binary data for each time field is spread across two nibbles. This scheme (as opposed to simple BCD) leaves some extra bits for encoding the SMPTE type (and for future use).

Now, let's convert our example time of 01:37:52:16 into Quarter Frame format, putting in the correct hexadecimal conversions:

```
F1 00
F1 11          10H = 16 decimal

F1 24
F1 33          34H = 52 decimal

F1 45
F1 52          25H = 37 decimal

F1 61
F1 76          01H = 01 decimal (SMPTE Type is 30 frames/non-drop)

(note: the value transmitted is "6" because the SMPTE Type
(11 binary) is encoded in bits 5 and 6)
```

For SMPTE Types of 24, 30 drop frame, and 30 non-drop frame, the frame number will always be even. For SMPTE Type of 25, the frame number may be even or odd, depending on which frame number the 8-message sequence had started. In this case, you can see where the MIDI Time Code frame number would alternate between even and odd every second.

MIDI Time Code will take a very small percentage of the MIDI bandwidth. The fastest SMPTE time rate is 30 frames per second. The specification is to send 4 messages per frame— in other words, a 2-byte message (640 microseconds) every 8.333 milliseconds. This takes 7.68% of the MIDI bandwidth — a reasonably small amount. Also, in the typical MIDI Time Code systems we have imagined, it would be rare that normal MIDI and MIDI Time Code would share the same MIDI bus at the same time.

FULL MESSAGE

Quarter Frame messages handle the basic running work of the system. But they are not suitable for use when equipment needs to be fast-forwarded or rewound, located or cued to a specific time, as sending them continuously at accelerated speeds would unnecessarily clog up or outrun the MIDI data lines. For these cases, Full Messages are used, which encode the complete time into a single message. After sending a Full Message, the time code generator can pause for any mechanical devices to shuttle (or "autolocate") to that point, and then resume running by sending quarter frame messages.

FULL MESSAGE — (10 bytes)

F0 7F <chan> 01 <sub-id> hr mn sc fr F7

F0 7F = Real Time Universal System Exclusive Header
<chan> = 7F (message intended for entire system)
01 = 'Long Form Time Code' ID
<sub-id> = 00 (Full time Code Message)
hr = hours and type: 0 yy zzzzzz

yy = type:
00 = 24 Frames/Second
01 = 25 Frames/Second
10 = 30 Frames/Second (drop frame)
11 = 30 Frames/Second (non-drop frame)
ZZZZZ = Hours (00->23)
mn = Minutes (00 —>59)
sc = Seconds (00 —>59)
fr = Frames (00 —>29)
F7 = EOX

The time code indicated in the Full Message takes effect on receipt of the first quarter frame message after the Full Message.

USER BITS

"User Bits" are 32 bits provided by SMPTE for special functions which vary with the application, and which can be programmed only from equipment especially designed for this purpose. Up to four characters or eight digits can be written. Examples of use are adding a date code or reel number to the tape. The User Bits tend not to change throughout a run of time code.

USER BIT MESSAGE — (15 BYTES)

F0 7F <chan> 01 <sub-id> u1 u2 u3 u4 u5 u6 u7 u8 u9 F7

F0 7F = Real Time Universal System Exclusive Header
<chan> = 7F (message intended for entire system)
01 = Long Form Time Code ID
<sub-id> = 01 (User Bits Message)
u1 = 0000aaaa
u2 = 0000bbbb
u3 = 0000cccc
u4 = 0000dddd
u5 = 0000eeee
u6 = 0000ffff
u7 = 0000gggg
u8 = 0000hhhh
u9 = 000000ii
F7 = EOX

These nibble fields decode in an 8-bit format: aaaabbbb ccccdddd eeeeffff gggghhhh ii. It forms 4, 8-bit characters, and a 2-bit Format Code. u1 through u8 correspond to SMPTE Binary Groups 1 through 8. u9 are the two Binary Group Flag Bits, as defined by SMPTE.

This message can be sent whenever the User Bits values must be transferred to any devices down the line. Note that the user Bits Message may be sent by the MIDI Time Code Converter at any time. It is not sensitive to any mode.

SET-UP MESSAGES

Set-Up Messages are used to address individual units in a system. (A "unit" can be a multitrack tape deck, a VTR, a special effects generator, MIDI sequencer, etc.)

Of 128 possible event types, 19 are currently defined.

SET-UP MESSAGES (13 BYTES PLUS ANY ADDITIONAL INFORMATION):

F0 7E <chan>04 st hr mn sc fr ff sl sm <add. info> F7

F0 7E = Non-Real Time Universal System Exclusive Header
<chan> = Channel number
04 = Time Code Set-Up ID
st = Set-Up Type

- 00 = Special
- 01 = Punch In points
- 02 = Punch Out points
- 03 = Delete Punch In point
- 04 = Delete Punch Out point
- 05 = Event Start points
- 06 = Event Stop points
- 07 = Event Start points with additional info.
- 08 = Event Stop points with additional info.
- 09 = Delete Event Start point
- 0A = Delete Event Stop point
- 0B = Cue points
- 0C = Cue points with additional info
- 0D = Delete Cue point
- 0E = Event Name in additional info

hr = hours and type: 0yy zzzzz
yy = type:

- 00 = 24 Frames/Second
- 01 = 25 Frames/Second
- 10 = 30 Frames/Second drop frame
- 11 = 30 Frames/Second non-drop frame

zzzzz = Hours (00-23)
mn = Minutes (00-59)
sc = Seconds (00-59)
fr = Frames (00-29)
ff = Fractional Frames (00-99)
sl, sm = Event Number (LSB first)
<add. info.>
F7 = EOX

DESCRIPTION OF SET-UP TYPES

00 **Special** refers to the Set-Up information that affects a unit globally (as opposed to individual tracks, sounds, programs, sequences, etc.). In this case, the Special Type takes the place of the Event Number.
Five are defined. Note that types 01 00 through 04 00 ignore the event time field.

00 00 **Time Code Offset** refers to a relative Time Code offset for each unit. For example, a piece of video and a piece of music that are supposed to go together may be created at different times, and more than likely have different absolute time code positions — therefore, one must be offset from the other so that they will match up. Just like there is one master time code for an entire system, each unit only needs one offset value per unit.

01 00 **Enable Event List** means for a unit to enable execution of events in its list if the appropriate MTC or SMPTE time occurs.

02 00 **Disable Event List** means for a unit to disable execution of its event list but not to erase it. This facilitates an MTC Event Manager in muting particular devices in order to concentrate on others in a complex system where many events occur simultaneously.

03 00 **Clear Event List** means for a unit to erase its entire event list.

04 00 **System Stop** refers to a time when the unit may shut down. This serves as a protection against Event Starts without matching Event Stops, tape machines running past the end of the reel, and so on.

01/02 **Punch In and Punch Out** refer to the enabling and disabling of record mode on a unit. The Event Number refers to the track to be recorded. Multiple punch in/punch out points (and any of the other event types below) may be specified by sending multiple Set-Up messages with different times.

03/04 **Delete Punch In or Out** deletes the matching point (time and event number) from the Cue List.

05/06 **Event Start and Stop** refer to the running or playback of an event, and imply that a large sequence of events or a continuous event is to be started or stopped. The event number refers to which event on the targeted slave is to be played. A single event number may have several pairs of Start and Stop times.

07/08 **Event Start and Stop with Additional Information** refer to an event (as above) with additional parameters transmitted in the Set-Up message between the Time and EOX. The additional parameters may take the form of an effects unit's internal parameters, the volume level of a sound effect, etc. See below for a description of additional information.

09/0A **Delete Event Start/Stop** means to delete the matching (event number and time) event (with or without additional information) from the Cue List.

0B **Cue Point** refers to individual event occurrences, such as marking "hit" points for sound effects, reference points for editing, and so on. Each Cue number may be assigned to a specific reaction, such as a specific one-shot sound event (as opposed to a continuous event, which is handled by Start/Stop).

0C **Cue Point with additional information** is exactly like Event Start/Stop with Additional information, except that the event represents a Cue Point rather than a Start/Stop Point.

0D **Delete Cue Point** means to Delete the matching (event number and time) Cue event with or without additional information from the Cue list.

0E **Event Name in Additional Information**. This merely assigns a name to a given event number. It is for human logging purposes. See Additional Information description.

EVENT TIME

This is the SMPTE/MIDI Time Code time at which the given event is supposed to occur. Actual time is in 1/100th frame resolution, for those units capable of handling bits or some other form of sub-frame resolution, and should otherwise be self explanatory.

EVENT NUMBER

This is a 14-bit value, enabling 16,384 of each of the above types to be individually addressed. "sl" is the 7 LS bits, and "sm" is the 7 MS bits.

ADDITIONAL INFORMATION DESCRIPTION

Additional information consists of a nibblized MIDI data stream, LS nibble first. The exception is Set-Up Type 0E, where the additional information is nibblized ASCII, LS nibble first. An ASCII newline is accomplished by sending CR and LF in the ASCII. CR alone functions solely as a carriage return, and LF alone functions solely as a Line-Feed.

For example, a MIDI Note On message such as 91 46 7F would be nibblized and sent as 01 and 09 06 04 0F 07. In this way, any device can decode any message regardless of who it was intended for. Device-specific messages should be sent as nibblized MIDI System Exclusive messages.

POTENTIAL PROBLEMS

There is a possible problem with MIDI merger boxes improperly handling the F1 message, since they do not currently know how many bytes are following. However, in typical MIDI Time Code systems, we do not anticipate applications where the MIDI Time Code must be merged with other MIDI signals occurring at the same time.

Please note that there is plenty of room for additional Set-Up types, etc., to cover unanticipated situations and configurations.

SIGNAL PATH SUMMARY

Data sent between the Master Time Code Source (which may be, for example, a Multitrack Tape Deck with a SMPTE Synchronizer) and the MIDI Time Code Converter is always SMPTE Time Code.

Data sent from the MIDI Time Converter to the Master Control/Cue Sheet (note that this may be a MTCC-equipped tape deck or mixing console as well as a cue-sheet) is **always MIDI Time Code.** The specific MIDI Time Code messages which are used depend on the current operating mode, as explained below:

Play Mode: The Master Time Code Source (tape deck) is in normal **PLAY MODE** at normal or vari-speed rates. The MIDI Time Code Converter is transmitting **Quarter Frame** ("F1") messages to the Master Control/Cue Sheet. The frame messages are in **ASCENDING** order, starting with "F1 0X" and ending with "F1 7X". If the tape machine is capable of play mode in **REVERSE**, then the frame messages will be transmitted in **REVERSE** sequence, starting with "F1 7X" and ending with "F1 0X".

Cue Mode: The Master Time Code Source is being "rocked," or "cued" by hand. The tape is still contacting the playback head so that the listener can cue, or preview the contents of the tape slowly. The MIDI Time Code Converter is transmitting **FRAME ("F1")** messages to the Master Control/Cue Sheet. If the tape is being played in the **FORWARD** direction, the frame messages are sent in **ASCENDING** order, starting with "F1 0X" and ending with "F1 7X". If the tape machine is played in the **REVERSE** direction, then the frame messages will be transmitted in **REVERSE** sequence, starting with "F1 7X" and ending with "F1 0X".

Because the tape is being moved by hand in Cue Mode, the tape direction can change quickly and often. The order of the Frame Message sequence must change along with the tape direction.

Fast-Forward/Rewind Mode: In this mode, the tape is in a high-speed wind or rewind, and is not touching the playback head. No "cueing" of the tapes material is going on. Since this is a "search" mode, synchronization of the Master Control/Cue Sheet is not as important as in the Play or Cue Mode. Thus, in this mode, the MIDI Time Code Converter only needs to send a "Full Message" every so often to the Cue Sheet. This acts as a rough indicator of the Master's position. The SMPTE time indicate by the "Full Message" actually takes effect upon the reception of the next "F1" quarter frame message (when "Play Mode" has resumed).

Shuttle Mode: This is just another expression for "Fast-Forward/Rewind Mode".

References and Credits

SMPTE 12M (ANSI V98.12M-19181).

Thanks to Stanley Jungleib for additional text. Also many thanks to all of the MMA and JMSC members for their suggestions and contributions to the MIDI Time Code Specification.

Introduction

In order to allow full access to a MIDI device, manufacturers should publish the formats of the System Exclusive messages used by their instruments. The format of these messages will vary from manufacturer to manufacturer. Often, even devices made by the same company will use different System Exclusive message formats.

Some manufacturers have standardized the general formats for the System Exclusive messages used by their product lines. This section contains all available Manufacturer's System Exclusive formats. In it you will find the general formats used by the following companies:

- Akai
- Casio
- Kawai
- Korg
- Roland
- Yamaha

Each manufacturer details message formats and communication protocols in slightly different ways. Since there is no standardized set of guidelines for presenting or detailing this data, it is presented here as it appeared in the original documents.

The MIDI System Exclusive Book contains a complete set of all available System Exclusive message formats (and in many cases, communication protocols and implementation details as well) for individual products made by the following manufacturers:

- Akai
- ART
- Casio
- E-mu Systems
- Ensoniq
- Fender
- JL Cooper
- Korg
- Lowrey
- Oberheim
- PPG
- Roland
- Sequential
- Siel
- Yamaha

Akai Exclusive Format

Version 1.0 May 9, 1986

1. GENERAL FORMAT

1.1 Message Structure

Value	Description
F0h	Status of exclusive message
47h	AKAI ID
UN#	Unit number
OP#	Operation number
FM#	Format number
EFM#	Extension of format number
[BL#]	Block number
[DATA]	
:	
:	
F7h	EOX (End of exclusive)

1.2 Unit Number (UN#)

Value	Description
00h - 0Fh	UN# + 1 = MIDI channel number

1.3 Operation Number (OP#)

	lower																
	U/L	0	1	2	3	4	5	6	7	8	9	A	B	C	D	E	F
upper	0																
	1																
	2																
	3																
	4	WSB	RQB	RNB		DAT	EOF								ACK	NAK	RJC
	5																
	6																
	7																

Name	Value	Description
WSB	40h	Want to send a block
RQB	41h	Request a block
RNB	42h	Request next block
DAT	44h	Data in block
EOF	45h	End of file
ACK	4Dh	Acknowledge
NAK	4Eh	Negative acknowledge
RJC	4Fh	Rejection

1.4 Format number (FM#)

	lower															
upper U/L	0	1	2	3	4	5	6	7	8	9	A	B	C	D	E	F
0																
1																
2	612															
3																
4																
5																
6																
7																

Name	Value	Description
612	20h	S612

2. MESSAGE FORMAT

2.1 WSB (Want to send a block)

No.	Value	Description
1	F0h	Status of exclusive message
2	47h	AKAI ID
3	UN#	Unit number
4	40h	WSB
5	FM#	Format number
6	EFM#	Extension of format number
[7	BL#]	Block number
8	F7h	EOX (End of exclusive)

2.2 RQB (Request a block)

No.	Value	Description
1	F0h	Status of exclusive message
2	47h	AKAI ID
3	UN#	Unit number
4	41h	RQB
5	FM#	Format number
6	EFM#	Extension of format number
[7	BL#]	Block number
8	F7h	EOX (End of exclusive)

2.3 RNB (Request next block)

No.	Value	Description
1	F0h	Status of exclusive message
2	47h	AKAI ID
3	UN#	Unit number
4	42h	RNB
5	FM#	Format number
6	EFM#	Extension of format number
7	F7h	EOX (End of exclusive)

2.4 DAT (Data in block)

No.	Value	Description
1	F0h	Status of exclusive
2	47h	AKAI ID
3	UN#	Unit number
4	44h	DAT
5	FM#	Format number
6	EFM#	Extension of format number
7	:	[data]
	:	
8	F7h	EOX (End of exclusive)

2.5 EOF (End of file)

No.	Value	Description
1	F0h	Status of exclusive
2	47h	AKAI ID
3	UN#	Unit number
4	45h	EOF
5	FM#	Format number
6	EFM#	Extension of format number
7	F7h	EOX (End of exclusive)

2.6 ACK (Acknowledge)

No.	Value	Description
1	F0h	Status of exclusive message
2	47h	AKAI ID
3	UN#	Unit number
4	4Dh	ACK
5	FM#	Format number
6	EFM#	Extension of format number
7	F7h	EOX (End of exclusive)

2.7 NAK (Negative Acknowledge)

No.	Value	Description
1	F0h	Status of exclusive message
2	47h	AKAI ID
3	UN#	Unit number
4	4Eh	NAK
5	FM#	Format number
6	EFM#	Extension of format number
7	F7h	EOX (End of exclusive)

2.8 RJC (Rejection)

No.	Value	Description
1	F0h	Status of exclusive message
2	47h	AKAI ID
3	UN#	Unit number
4	4Fh	RJC
5	FM#	Format number
6	EFM#	Extension of format number
7	F7h	EOX (End of exclusive)

3. Operation Examples

3.1 Send A File

3.1.1 Fundamental Procedure

This Unit	Message	Objective Unit
	DAT ----->	

3.1.2 WSB Procedure

3.1.2.1

This Unit	Message	Objective Unit
	WSBx ----->	
	<-----ACK	
	DATx ----->	
	<-----ACK	
	DATx+1 --->	
	<-----ACK	
	:	
	:	
	DATn ----->	
	<-----ACK	
	EOF ----->	
	<-----ACK	
		x : BL# (0-7Fh)

3.1.2.2

This Unit	Message	Objective Unit
	WSBx ————>	
	<————ACK	
	DATx ————>	
	<————ACK	
	DATx+1 ——>	
	<————ACK	
	:	
	:	
	DATn ————>	
	<————EOF	
	ACK ————>	

3.1.2.3

If number of data fixed, following procedure is permitted.

This Unit	Message	Objective Unit
	WSBx ————>	
	<————ACK	
	DATx ————>	
	<————ACK	
	DATx+1 ——>	
	<————ACK	
	:	
	:	
	DATn ————>	
	<————ACK	

This Unit	Message	Objective Unit
	WSBx ————>	
	<————ACK	
	DATx ————>	
	<————ACK	
	WSBx+1 ——>	
	<————ACK	
	DATx+1 ——>	
	<————ACK	
	:	
	:	
	WSBn ————>	
	<————ACK	
	DATn ————>	
	<————ACK	

3.2. REQUEST A FILE

3.2.1 Fundamental Procedure

This Unit	Message	Objective Unit
	<———— DAT	

3.2.2 RQB Procedure

3.2.2.1

This Unit	Message	Objective Unit
	RQBx ————>	
	<————DATx	
	RNB ————>	
	<————DATx+1	
	:	
	:	
	RNB ————>	
	<————DATn	
	RNB ————>	
	<————EOF	
	ACK ————>	

3.2.2.2

This Unit	Message	Objective Unit
	RQBx ————>	
	<————DATx	
	RNB ————>	
	<————DATx+1	
	:	
	:	
	RNB ————>	
	<————DATn	
	EOF ————>	
	<————ACK	

3.2.2.3

If number of data fixed, following procedure is permitted.

This Unit	Message	Objective Unit
	RQBx ————>	
	<————DATx	
	RQBx+1 ——>	
	<————DATx+1	
	:	
	:	
	RQBn ————>	
	<————DATn	
	ACK ————>	

3.3 NAK, RJC PROCEDURE

3.3.1

```
This Unit         Message                  Objective Unit
---------------------------------------------------------
                  WSBx      ————>
                   <————ACK
                  DATx      ————>
                   <————NAK
                  DATx      ————>
                   <————ACK
                  DATx+1      ——>
                   <————ACK
                        :
                        :
```

3.3.2

```
This Unit         Message                  Objective Unit
---------------------------------------------------------
                  WSBx      ————>
                   <————ACK
                  DATx      ————>
                   <————NAK
                (  DATx      ————>        )
                (   <————NAK              )
                  RJC ————>
```

3.3.3

```
This Unit         Message                  Objective Unit
---------------------------------------------------------
                  WSBx      ————>
                   <————NAK
```

3.3.4

```
This Unit         Message                  Objective Unit
---------------------------------------------------------
                  RQBx      ————>
                   <————DATx
                  RNB       ————>
                   <————DATx+1
                  NAK       ————>
                   <————DATx+1
                  RNB       ————>
                   <————DATx+2
                        :
```

3.3.5

```
This Unit      Message                Objective Unit
--------------------------------------------------
               RQBx      ---->
                <----DATx
               RNB       ---->
                <----DATx+1
         (     NAK       ---->        )
         (      <----DATx+1           )
               RJC ---->
```

3.3.6

```
This Unit      Message                Objective Unit
--------------------------------------------------
               RQBx      ---->
```

** note **

When the transfer sequence is discontinued, RJC must be sent.
When the unit receives RJC, then operation of the unit should quit.

Casio MIDI System Exclusive Format

June 6, 1986

The data format for the CASIO's exclusive message is divided into two main categories:
[1] Hand Shake Type
[2] Non Hand Shake Type

Hand shake type is applied for the bulk data transfer (such as sound data and sequencer data, etc.)

Non hand shake type is applied for functional control (like glide on/off).

(1) Hand Shake Type

There are two types of messages.

(1) Data send request

For example:

The musical instrument A requests to the musical instrument B, then, the instrument B sends out the bulk data, and then, the instrument A receives that data.

General Format

```
Musical Instrument A:              Musical Instrument B

F0 ii jj jj 7n xx vv
(request command)      ------------>
                                      F0 ii jj jj 7n 30
                       <------------  (ready)
7n 31
(continue)             ------------>
                                      0l 0h 0l 0h  .... (7n 32)
                       <------------  (bulk data)     (block end)
(7n 31)
(continue)             ------------>
                                      0l 0h 0l 0h
                       <------------  (bulk data).... F7
F7
(EOX)                  ------------>
```

ii: CASIO id , Hex '44'
jjjj: Sub ID (CZ Synthesizer : Hex '0000')
n: Basic channel
xx: Send request command
vv: data of command
l: bulk data (4-bit lower part of 1 byte data)
h: bulk data (4-bit higher part of 1 byte data)

(2) Data receive request

For example:

The musical instrument A requests to the musical instrument B, then, the instrument A sends out the bulk data, and then, the instrument B receives that data.

General Format

Musical Instrument A		Musical Instrument B
F0 ii jj jj 7n xx vv (request command)	——————>	
	<——————	F0 ii jj jj 7n 30 (ready)
0l 0h 0l 0h . . . . (7n 32) (bulk data) (block end)	——————>	
	<——————	(7n 30) (ready)
0l 0h 0l 0h . . . . F7 (bulk data)	——————>	
	<——————	F7

ii: CASIO id , Hex '44'
jjjj: Sub id (CZ Synthesizer : Hex '0000')
n: Basic channel
xx: Receive request command
vv: data of command
l: bulk data (4-bit lower part of 1 byte data)
h: bulk data (4-bit higher part of 1 byte data)

(2) Non Hand Shake Type

General format

F0 ii jj jj 7n xx vv vv . . F7

ii: CASIO id, hex '44'
jjjj: Sub ID (CZ synthesizer : Hex '0000')
n: Basic channel or Voice channel
xx: command
vv..: data of command

Command Example:

- bend width
- transpose
- tone mix
- glide note
- glide time
- glide on/off
- modulation depth
- sound level
- portament sweep
- cartridge on/off
- modulation after touch depth
- cursor
- page
- poly number
- split point
- time break
- key code sweep
- others

*please refer the CZ-5000 synthesizer exclusive manual.

October 11, 1985

NO.	DESCRIPTION	VALUE	
1	Exclusive	F0H	
2	KAWAI ID	40H	
3	Channel no.	0nH	n = 0-FH
4	Function no.	0 - 7FH	see Note 2
5	Group no.	0 - 7FH	see Note 2
6	Machine no.	0 - 7FH	see Note 3
7	data	0 - 7FH	
8	data	0 - 7FH	
*	data	0 - 7FH	
*	data	0 - 7FH	
*	data	0 - 7FH	
*	EOX	F7H	

Note 1 — The above chart is KAWAI MIDI Exclusive Format. Only Machine ID REQUEST, having no Group number and Machine number message, is concluded at the fourth byte followed by EOX.

Note 2 — Function and Group number are listed in Table 1, and 2, respectively.

Note 3 — Machine no. is the ID of an instrument. For example synthesizer K-3 is 01H.

Table 1 Function Number

Function no.	Description
00H	One Block Data REQUEST
01H	All Block Data REQUEST
02H - 0FH	Undefined
10H	Parameter Send
11H - 1FH	Undefined
20H	One Block Data DUMP
21H	All Block Data DUMP
22H - 3FH	Undefined
40H	Write Complete
41H	Write Error
42H	Write Error by protect
43H	Write Error by no cartridge
44H - 5FH	Undefined
60H	Machine ID REQUEST
61H	Machine ID ACKNOWLEDGE
62H - 7FH	Undefined

Table 2 Group Number

Group no.	Group Name
00H	Synthesizer
01H	Organ
02H	Drum Machine
03H	Sequencer
04H - 7FH	Undefined

Korg MIDI Exclusive Data Format

1. BASIC FORMAT

Though an exclusive formation of each equipment will be adopted as the format following DEVICE ID, its basic style is as follows.

STATUS	KORG ID	FORMAT	DEVICE	DATA	DATA	EOX
FOH	42H	ID	ID			F7H

(DEVICE ID through DATA:) This part is different depending on FORMAT ID

Kind of FORMAT ID;

20 H: Based on our own MESSAGE FORMAT.
21 H: Not based on our own MESSAGE FORMAT (No channel function).
3n H: Not based on our own MESSAGE FORMAT (Channel function n = 0 - F : Basic Channel).
4n H: DEVICE ID REQUEST (Channel function n=0-F : Basic Channel).

2. FORMAT ID : 20 H

There is no item adopting it at present (as of June 5, 1986).

3. FORMAT ID : 21 H

Formats mainly for DATA DUMP.

1. DATA DUMP REQUEST

STATUS	KORG ID	FORMAT ID	DEVICE	FUNCTION CODE	EOX
FOH	42 H	21 H	ID	10 H	F7H

2. DATA ERROR MESSAGE

STATUS	KORG ID	FORMAT ID	DEVICE	FUNCTION CODE	EOX
FOH	42 H	21 H	ID	20H	F7H

3. DUMP DATA

STATUS	KORG ID	FORMAT	DEVICE	DATA	DATA	EOX
FOH	42H	21	ID			F7H

4. FORMAT ID : 3n H

4-1. FORMAT

Though an exclusive formation of each equipment will be adopted as the format following DEVICE ID, its style is basically as follows.

STATUS	KORG ID	FORMAT ID	DEVICE	FUNCTION	*1	EOX
FO H	42	3n H	ID	CODE	DATA..	F7H

*1 In some occasions, there will be no DATA BYTE depending on the function code, the length of DATA BYTE is changeable.

4-2. Kind of FUNCTION CODE

Though assignment of FUNCTION CODE will be done as follows, it is not a definitive one, but changeable.

00 H - 1 F H : REQUEST
20 H - 3 F H : MESSAGE
40 H - 7 F H : DATA

See a function code list.

5) FORMAT ID : 4n H

This FORMAT ID is itself a special code for which DEVICE ID REQUEST function is provided, and used when DEVICE ID of the equipment is requested to send. The equipment which received this code should send the following messages.

STATUS F0H	KORG ID 42 H	FORMAT ID 3n H	DEVICE ID	EOX F7H

FORMAT ID 3nH. FUNCTION CODE LIST

	REQUEST		MESSAGE		DATA
L/H	0	1	2	3	4
0		Program Parameter Save Req.	Dump Error		Program Parameter
1		Write Req.	Write Completed		Program Parameter Change
2		Mode Req.	Write Error		Mode Data
3		Play Mode Req.	Data Load Completed		PCM Data
4		PCM Data Save Req.	Data Load Error		Multi Sound Parameter
5		Multi Sound Parameter Save Req.			Multi Sound List Data
6		Multi Sound List Data Save Req.			Program List
7		Parameter Name List Save Req.			SEQ Data
8		All SEQ Data Req.			
9					
A					
B					
C		All Tone Dump Req.			All Tone Dump
D					
E					
F					Data End Block

Roland MIDI Exclusive Format

June 11, 1986

1. GENERAL FORMAT

1.1 MESSAGE STRUCTURE

Value	Description
F0H	Status of exclusive message
41H	Roland ID
OP	Operation code * note 1
UN#	Unit number
FT	Format type * note 1
[DATA]	(Data structure is dependent on FT* note 2)
F7H	EOX (End of Exclusive)

* Note 1:

Number of the data bytes should not exceed 256. (except sum)

(OP)
(or 00H 00H .... OP)
(--- n bytes of 00H ---)

* Note 2 :

Receiver's routine should recognize the value 00H in OP or FT as an extension.

1.2 OPERATION CODE

lower ---->

	U¥L	0	1	2	3	4	5	6	7	A	B	C	D	E	F
u	0	EXT													
p	1														
p	2														
e	3	PRC	MNC	IPC		PGR	APR	IPR	BLD						
r	4	WSF	RQF	DAT	ACK		EOF							ERR	RJC
	5	WSF	RQF	DAT	PAS	CNT	EOF		HDO						
	6	GOO													
	7	RJC	ERR												

Name	Value	Description		
EXT	00H	: Extension		
APP	30H	: All parameters of preset tone	(without FT)	*note 3
APM	31H	: All parameters of manual	(without FT)	*note 3
IPM	32H	: Individual parameter of manual	(without FT)	*note 3
PGR	34H	: Program number		
APR	35H	: All parameters		
IPR	36H	: Individual parameter		
BLD	37H	: Bulk dump		
WSF	40H	: Want to send a file		
RQF	41H	: Request a file		
DAT	42H	: Data in file		
ACK	43H	: Acknowledge		
EOF	45H	: End of file		
ERR	4EH	: Communication Error		
RJC	4FH	: Rejection		
WSF	50H	: Want to send a file	(without UN#, FT)	*note 4
RQF	51H	: Request a file	(without UN#, FT)	*note 4
DAT	52H	: Data header	(without UN#)	*note 4
PAS	53H	: Request next data	(without UN#, FT)	*note 4
CNT	54H	: Continue	(without UN#, FT)	*note 4
EOF	55H	: End of file	(without UN#, FT)	*note 4
HDO	57H	: Data header (one way, without UN#)		*note 5
GOO	60H	: No communication error		*note 4
RJC	70H	: Rejection	(without UN#, FT)	*note 4
ERR	71H	: Communication Error	(without UN#, FT)	*note 4

* Note 3: Used by JUNO-106, MKS-7, and MKB-200
* Note 4: Used by TR-909, TR-707, and TR-727
* Note 5: Used by MSQ-100

1.3 UNIT NUMBER

UN#

00H - 0FH : = MIDI basic channel
10H - 1FH : = MIDI basic channel (Representative)
20H - 7EH : True unit number
7FH : For unit which does not have the MIDI basic channel and the true unit number.

1.4 FORMAT TYPE

	lower---->																
	U¥L	0	1	2	3	4	5	6	7	8	9	A	B	C	D	E	F
u	0	EXT	TR9	TR7		TR5											
p	1																
p	2	KS8	JX8	DD3	AJU	JX0											
e	3																
r	4																
	5	SD2	SR2														
	6	SB8															
	7	SQ1															

EXT : Extension
TR9 : TR-909
KS8 : MKS-80
AJU : JU-1, JU-2, HS-10, HS-80, PG-300
JX0 : JX-10
SD2 : SDE-2500
SB8 : SBX-80

TR7 : TR-707, TR-727
JX8 : JX-8P
SR2 : SRV-2000
SQ1 : MSQ-100
TR5 : TR-505
DD3 : DDR-30

2. ONE WAY TRANSFER

Operation Code

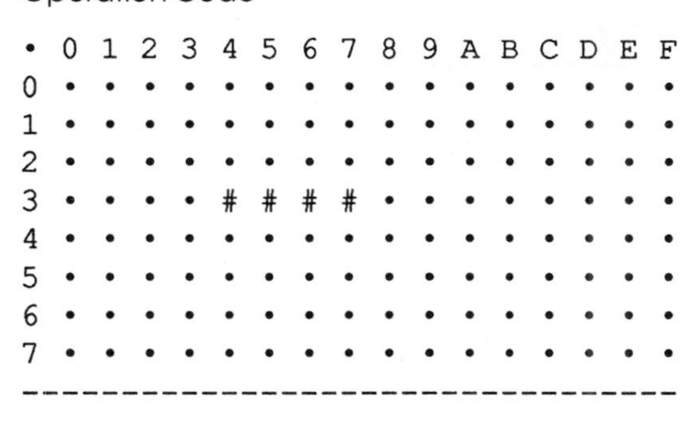

```
• 0 1 2 3 4 5 6 7 8 9 A B C D E F
0 • • • • • • • • • • • • • • • •
1 • • • • • • • • • • • • • • • •
2 • • • • • • • • • • • • • • • •
3 • • • • # # # # • • • • • • • •
4 • • • • • • • • • • • • • • • •
5 • • • • • • • • • • • • • • • •
6 • • • • • • • • • • • • • • • •
7 • • • • • • • • • • • • • • • •
---------------------------------
```

2.1 MESSAGE TYPES

2.1.1 Program number PGR

```
F0H     <—   Exclusive
41H     <—   Roland ID
34H     <—   Operation code
UN#     <—   Unit number
FT      <—   Format type
LV#     <—   Level of program number              *note 6
GR#     <—   Group number   ( 0 - 7FH )           *note 7
EP#     <—   Extension of program number          *note 8
PG#     <—   Program number
FN#     <—   Function number                      *note 9
F7H     <—   EOX  ( End of exclusive )
```

2.1.2 All Parameters APR

When the number is changed.
(Level 1 : Tone button is pressed. (group, bank, tone etc.))
(Level 2 : Patch button is pressed.)

```
F0H     <—   Exclusive
41H     <—   Roland ID
35H     <—   Operation code
UN#     <—   Unit number
FT      <—   Format type
LV#     <—   Level of program number              *note 6
GR#     <—   Group number   ( 0 - 7FH )           *note 7
vvH     <—   value   ( 0 - 7FH )
  :
  :
F7H     <—   EOX  ( End of Exclusive )
```

2.1.3 Individual Parameter IPR

When the parameter in level one is changed.
(Level 1: Tone parameter is changed.(LFO rate, VCF cutoff etc.))
(Level 2 : Patch parameter is changed.)

```
F0H     <—   Exclusive
41H     <—   Roland ID
36H     <—   Operation code
UN#     <—   Unit number
FT      <—   Format type
LV#     <—   Level of program number              *note 6
GR#     <—   Group number   ( 0 - 7FH )           *note 7

[ PR#   <—   Parameter number   ( 0 - 7FH )
vvH   ] <—   value   ( 0 - 7FH )

[    :        ]                   **
[    :        ]                   **
F7H     <—   EOX  ( End of exclusive )
```

** [ ]   are optional.

2.1.4 Bulk dump BLD

```
F0H      <—   Exclusive
41H      <—   Roland ID
37H      <—   Operation code
UN#      <—   Unit number
FT       <—   Format type
LV#      <—   Level of program number              *note 6
GR#      <—   Group number   ( 0 - 7FH )           *note 7
EP#      <—   Extension of program number          *note 8
PG#      <—   Program number
vvH      <—   value   ( 0 - 7FH )
 :
 :
F7H      <—   EOX  ( End of exclusive )
```

* Note 6: LV#

20H	: Level 1 (PG# indicates tone number, values are tone parameters.)
30H	: Level 2 (PG# indicates patch number, values are patch parameters.)

* Note 7: GR#

In level 1 --

00H	: Any tone group (used only by MPG-80)
01H	: Tone group 1 (ex. Upper)
02H	: Tone group 2 (ex. Lower)

In level 2 --

00H	: Any patch group (used only by MPG-80)
01H	: Patch group 1 (ex. Upper)
02H	: Patch group 2 (ex. Lower)

In level 3 --

00H	: Any bank group
01H	: Bank group 1 (ex. Bank 1)
02H	: Bank group 2 (ex. Bank 2)

* Note 8 : EP#

00H	: Next byte (PG#) indicates tone or patch number.
01H - 7EH	: Reserved for future.
7FH	: ID of manual mode.

* Note 9 : FN#

00H	: NOP
01H	: Read data (shown by the program number) from memory and set.
02H	: Write data to memory with the program number.
03H - 7FH	: Reserved for future.

2.2 OPERATION EXAMPLES

When the Tone-Number is changed.

1: PGN (Program number with NOP function)

```
F0H     <—   Exclusive
41H     <—   Roland ID
34H     <—   Operation code
UN#     <—   Unit number
FT      <—   Format type
20H     <—   Level 1
GR#     <—   Group number   ( 0  -  7FH )
00H     <—   PG# indicates the tone number
PG#     <—   Tone number
00H     <—   NOP
F7H     <—   EOX  ( End of exclusive )
```

2: APR (All parameter (Level 1))

```
F0H     <—   Exclusive
41H     <—   Roland ID
35H     <—   Operation code
UN#     <—   Unit number
FT      <—   Format type
20H     <—   Level 1
GR#     <—   Group number   ( 0  -  7FH )
vvH     <—   value  ( 0  -  7FH )
   :
   :
F7H     <—   EOX  ( End Of Exclusive )
```

When the Tone-Parameter is changed.

1: IPR (Individual parameter (Level 1))

```
 F0H     <—   Exclusive
 41H     <—   Roland ID
 36H     <—   Operation code
 UN#     <—   Unit number
 FT      <—   Format type
 20H     <—   Level 1
 GR#     <—   Group number (0  -  7FH )

[ PR#    <—   Parameter number (0  -  7FH )
 vvH   ] <—   value (0  -  7FH )

[  :     ]
[  :     ]
 F7H     <—   EOX  ( End of exclusive )
```

When the Patch-Number is changed

1: PGN (Program number with NOP function)

```
F0H     <—  Exclusive
41H     <—  Roland ID
34H     <—  Operation code
UN#     <—  Unit number
FT      <—  Format type
30H     <—  Level 2
00H     <—  dummy
00H     <—  PG# indicates the patch number
PG#     <—  Patch number
00H     <—  NOP
F7H     <—  EOX  ( End of exclusive )
```

2: APR (All parameter (Level 2))

```
F0H     <—  Exclusive
41H     <—  Roland ID
35H     <—  Operation code
UN#     <—  Unit number
FT      <—  Format type
30H     <—  Level 2
00H     <—  dummy
vvH     <—  value  ( 0  -  7FH )
  :
  :
F7H     <—  EOX  ( End Of Exclusive )
```

When the Patch-Parameter is changed.

1: IPR (Individual parameter (Level 2))

```
  F0H     <—  Exclusive
  41H     <—  Roland ID
  36H     <—  Operation code
  UN#     <—  Unit number
  FT      <—  Format type
  30H     <—  Level  2
  00H     <—  dummy
[ PR#     <—  Parameter number ( 0  -  7FH )
  vvH   ] <—  value ( 0  -  7FH )
[   :      ]
[   :      ]
  F7H     <—  EOX  ( End of exclusive )
```

3. HANDSHAKING COMMUNICATION

Operation Code

```
• 0 1 2 3 4 5 6 7 8 9 A B C D E F
0 • • • • • • • • • • • • • • • •
>
3 • • • • • • • • • • • • • • • •
4 # # # # • # • • • • • • • • # #
5 • • • • • • • • • • • • • • • •
>
7 • • • • • • • • • • • • • • • •
----------------------------------
```

3.1 MESSAGE TYPE

3.1.1 Want To Send A File WSF 40H

```
F0H     <—  Exclusive
41H     <—  Roland ID
40H     <—  Operation code
UN#     <—  Unit number
FT      <—  Format type
 :      <—  [   file name    ] *note 10
sum     <—  check sum
F7H     <—  EOX  ( End of exclusive )
```

3.1.2 Request A File RQF 41H

```
F0H     <—  Exclusive
41H     <—  Roland ID
41H     <—  Operation code
UN#     <—  Unit number
FT      <—  Format type
 :      <—  [   file name    ] *note 10
sum     <—  check sum
F7H     <—  EOX  ( End of exclusive )
```

3.1.3 Data DAT 42H

```
F0H     <—  Exclusive
41H     <—  Roland ID
42H     <—  Operation code
UN#     <—  Unit number
FT      <—  Format type
 :      <—  [   data   ]       *note 11
sum     <—  check sum
F7H     <—  EOX  ( End of exclusive )
```

3.1.4 Acknowledge ACK 43H

```
F0H     <—  Exclusive
41H     <—  Roland ID
43H     <—  Operation code
UN#     <—  Unit number
FT      <—  Format type
F7H     <—  EOX  ( End of exclusive )
```

3.1.5 End of file EOF 45H

```
F0H      <—   Exclusive
41H      <—   Roland ID
45H      <—   Operation code
UN#      <—   Unit number
FT       <—   Format type
F7H      <—   EOX  ( End of exclusive )
```

3.1.6 Communication error ERR 4EH

```
F0H      <—   Exclusive
41H      <—   Roland ID
4EH      <—   Operation code
UN#      <—   Unit number
FT       <—   Format type
F7H      <—   EOX  ( End of exclusive )
```

3.1.7 Rejection RJC 4FH

```
F0H      <—   Exclusive
41H      <—   Roland ID
4FH      <—   Operation code
UN#      <—   Unit number
FT       <—   Format type
F7H      <—   EOX  ( End of exclusive )
```

* Note 10:

```
[    file name    ] sum
--- 1 - 256 bytes ---
-------------------------
```

Summed value of the all bytes in data and sum
must be 00H (7 bits).

An exception:
If there is no 'file name', there must not be 'sum'.

Examples
FOH 41H 40H UN# FT F7H
FOH 41H 40H UN# FT 'file name' sum F7H

* Note 11

```
[      data      ] sum
--- 0 - 256 bytes ---
--------------------------
```

Summed value of the all bytes in data and sum
must be 00H (7 bits).

3.2 OPERATION EXAMPLES

3.2.1 When the unit wants to send a file.

This unit	Message	Objective unit
	WSF ————>	
	<———— ACK	
	DAT ————>	
	<———— ACK	
	:	
	:	
	DAT ————>	
	<———— ACK	
	EOF ————>	
	<———— ACK	

3.2.2 When the unit wants a file.

This unit	Message	Objective unit
	RQF ————>	
	<———— DAT	
	ACK ————>	
	:	
	:	
	<———— DAT	
	ACK ————>	
	<———— EOF	
	ACK ————>	

3.2.3 When the unit received a WSF message.

This unit	Message	Objective unit
	<———— WSF	
	ACK ————>	
	<———— DAT	
	ACK ————>	
	:	
	:	
	<———— DAT	
	ACK ————>	
	<———— EOF	
	ACK ————>	

3.2.4 When the unit received a RQF message.

```
This unit            Message              Objective unit

                     <———— RQF
                     DAT ————>
                     <———— ACK
                        :
                        :
                     DAT ————>
                     <———— ACK
                     EOF ————>
                     <———— ACK
```

3.2.5 When the unit received a ERR message.

```
This unit            Message              Objective unit

                     DAT ————>
                     <———— ACK
                       :
                       :
                     DATn————>
                     <———— ERR
          (          DATn————>            )
          (          <———— ERR            )
                     RJC ————>
```

* Note 12:

When the file transfer sequence is discontinued,RJC must be sent. When the unit receives RJC, then operation of the unit should be quit.

Issued June 1, 1986

GENERAL FORMAT

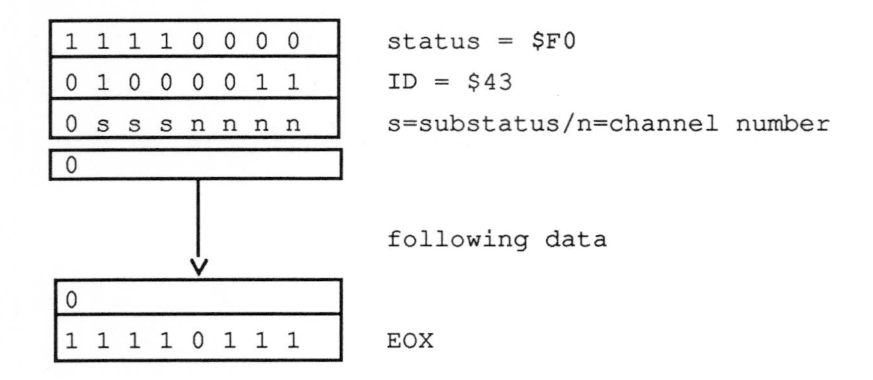

TABLE OF SUBSTATUS

s	substatus	Ref. Page
0	BULK DUMP	121
1	PARAMETER CHANGE	126
2	DUMP REQUEST	127
3	undefined	
4	undefined	
5	undefined	
6	MESSAGE	128
7	INSTRUMENT CLASSIFIED EXCLUSIVE	129

Note 1) ID = $43 (67) is YAMAHA's ID code.
2) Data format and data size of "following data" area are specified by substatus.
3) Channel number "n" may be same as receive channel of channel information or may be different from it. In the latter case, it may be called as "device number".

BULK DUMP

Substatus = 0

FORMAT

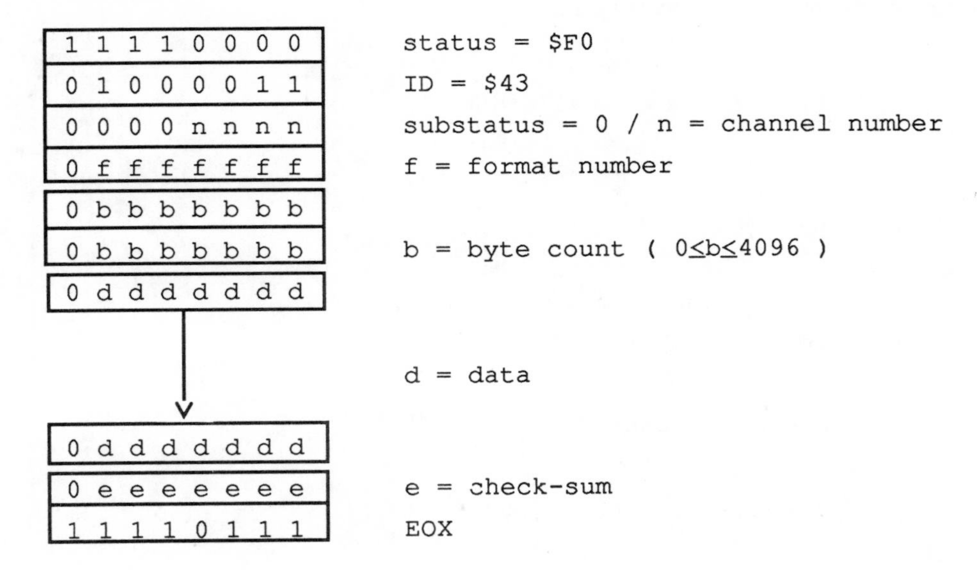

Note 1) This format is used for transmission of bulk data (more than one byte data block).
2) Format number "f" specifies data format and data size.
3) Check-sum is 2's complement of 7 bits sum of all data bytes.

SUBSTATUS = 0, f = 10 **SEQUENCE DUMP**

FORMAT

1 1 1 1 0 0 0 0	status = $F0
0 1 0 0 0 0 1 1	ID = $43
0 0 0 0 n n n n	n = channel number
0 0 0 0 1 0 1 0	format number = $A (10)
0 b b b b b b b	
0 b b b b b b b	b = byte count (10≤b≤4096)
0 a a a a a a a	
↓	a = classification name (ASCII - 4 chars.)
0 a a a a a a a	
0 m m m m m m m	
↓	m = sequence format name (ASCII - 6 chars.)
0 m m m m m m m	
0 d d d d d d d	
↓	d = data
0 d d d d d d d	
0 e e e e e e e	e = check-sum
1 1 1 1 0 1 1 1	EOX

Note 1) This bulk data format is used for transmission of variable length sequence data.
(example) SEQUENCER, RHYTHM PATTERN etc.

2) The format of the data is dependent on "m" (data format name).

SUBSTATUS = 0, f = 11 **RHYTHM PARAMETER DUMP**

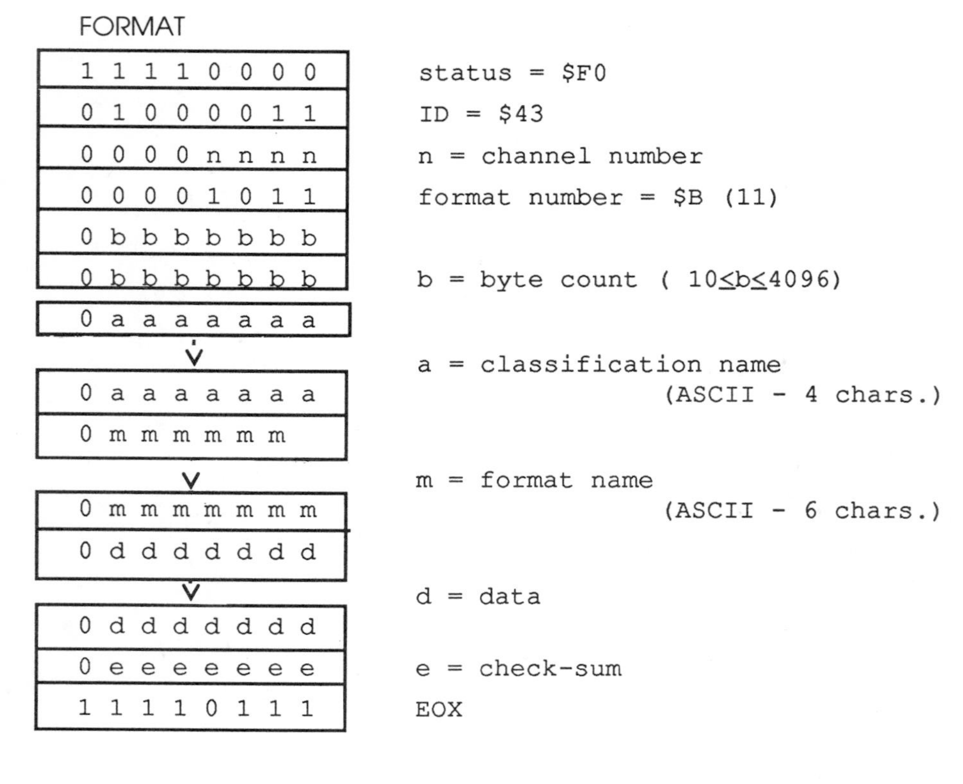

Note 1) This bulk data format is used for transmission of variable length control parameters of rhythm instrument. Rhythm pattern data should be transmitted by format f = 10 (SEQUENCE DUMP).

2) The format of the data is dependent on "m" (data format name).

SUBSTATUS = 0, f = 123 **UNIVERSAL BULK DUMP with FILE NAME**

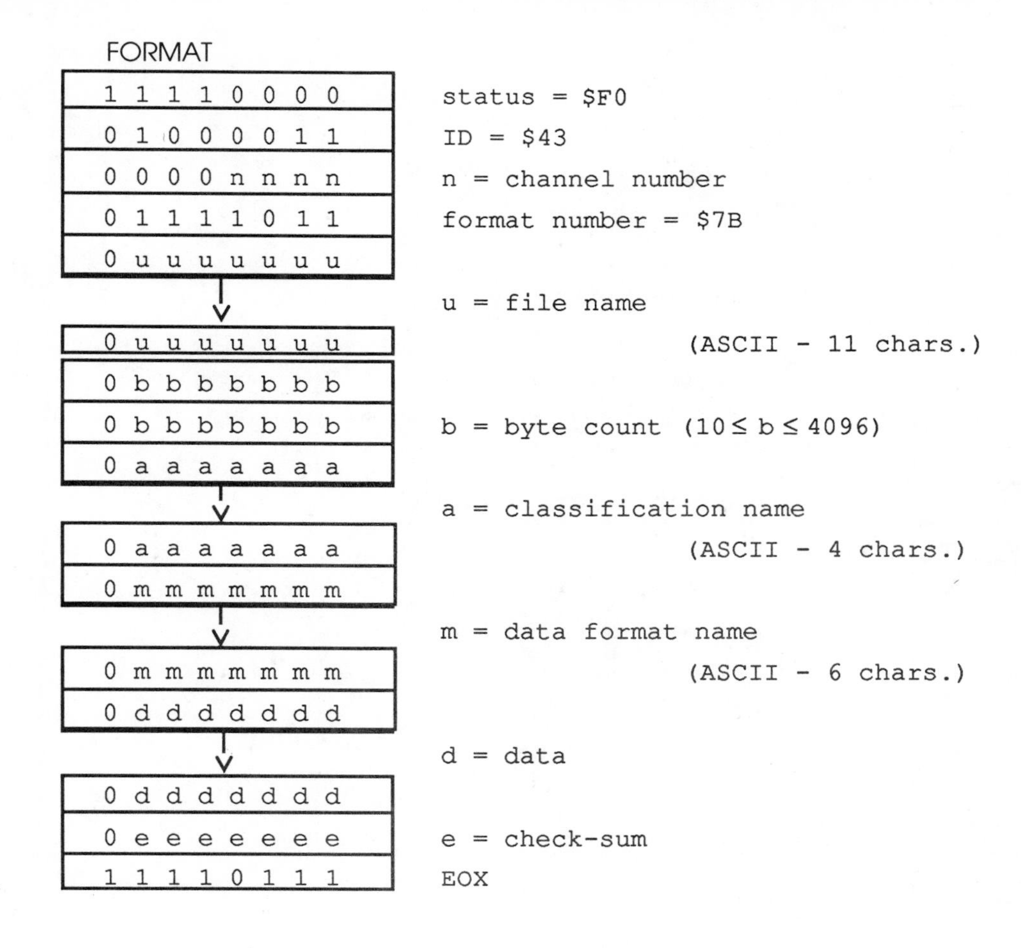

Note 1) This bulk data format is used for transmission of variable length data with a specified file name.

2) The format of file name is below;

byte 1 - 8 ; file name 8 chars.
byte 9 - 11; extension 3 chars.
total 11 bytes

3) The format of the data is dependent on "m" (data format name).

4) Check-sum is 2's complement of 7-bit sum of 10 bytes header and all of data bytes.

SUBSTATUS = 0, f = 124 **CONDITION SETUP**

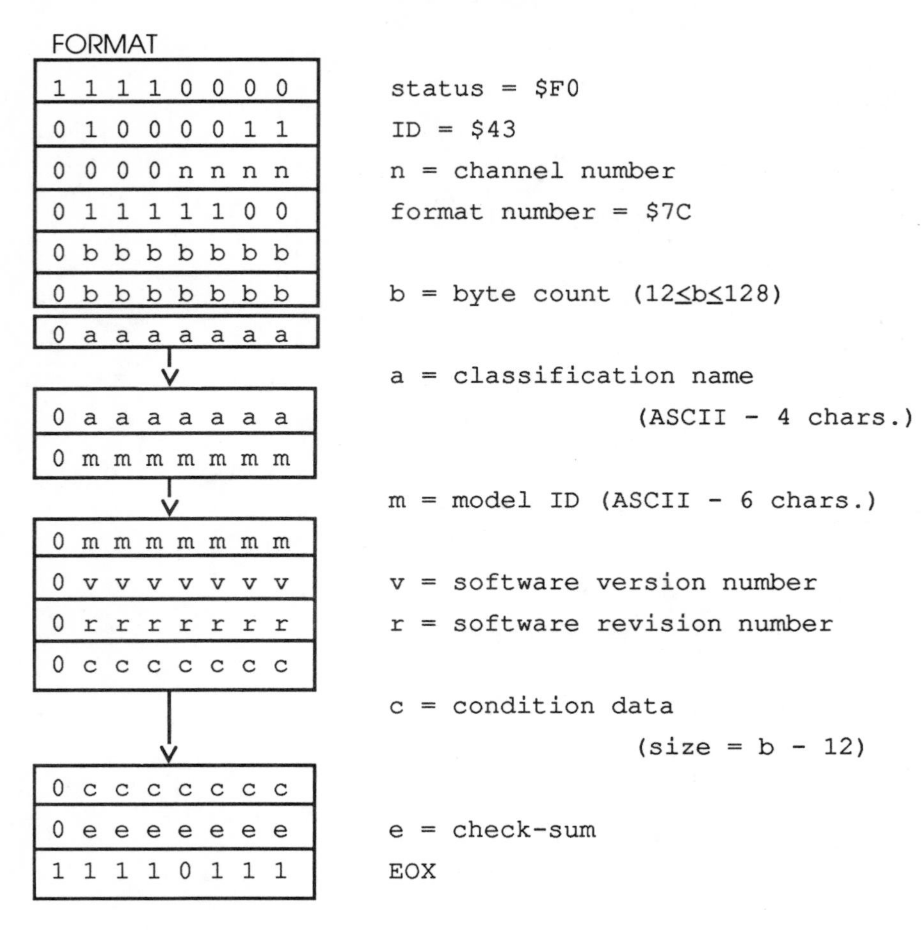

Note 1) This bulk data format is used for instantaneous setup of all panel and internal condition of the receiver.

2) classification = section name
model ID = development number of the model

(example) DX5 version 2.1
$4C,4D,20,20,38,39,33,33,20,20,02,01
L M - - 8 9 3 3 - - 2 1

SUBSTATUS = 0, f = 125 **CONDITION ACKNOWLEDGE**

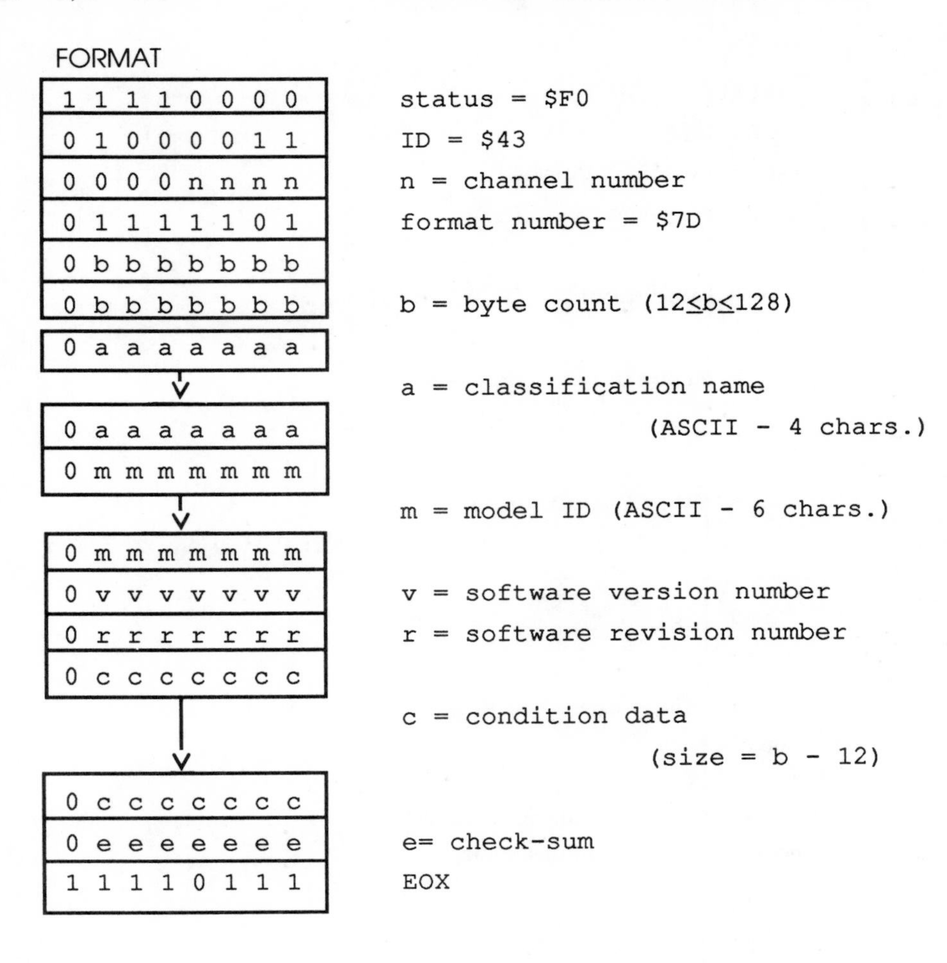

Note 1) This bulk data format is used for acknowledgement of panel and internal condition of the transmitter. When the receiver gets "CONDITION REQUEST", then it should transmit its condition by this data format.

2) classification = section name
model ID = development number of the model
(example) DX5 version 2.1
$4C,4D,20,20,38,39,33,33,20,20,02,01
L M - - 8 9 3 3 - - 2 1

SUBSTATUS = 0, f = 126 **UNIVERSAL BULK DUMP**

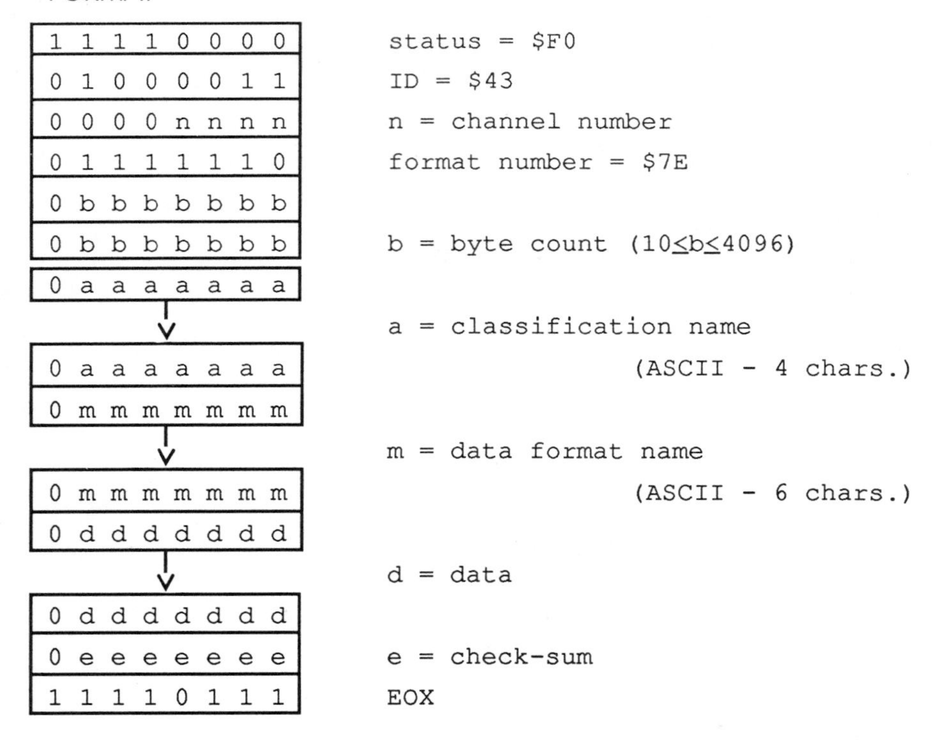

Note 1) This bulk data format is used for transmission of variable length data.
2) The format of the data is dependent on "m" (data format name).

PARAMETER CHANGE

SUBSTATUS = 1

FORMAT

1 1 1 1 0 0 0 0	status = $F0
0 1 0 0 0 0 1 1	ID = $43
0 0 0 1 n n n n	n = channel number
0 g g g g g h h	g = group / h = subgroup
0 p p p p p p p	p = parameter number
0 d d d d d d d	d = data
↓	
0 d d d d d d d	
1 1 1 1 0 1 1 1	EOX

Note 1) This format is used for transmission of single parameter.
2) Data size is specified by parameter number g, h and p.

DUMP REQUEST

SUBSTATUS = 2

FORMAT A

1 1 1 1 0 0 0 0	status = $F0
0 1 0 0 0 0 1 1	ID = $43
0 0 1 0 n n n n	substatus = 2 / n = channel number
0 f f f f f f f	f = format number
1 1 1 1 0 1 1 1	EOX

FORMAT B

1 1 1 1 0 0 0 0	status = $F0
0 1 0 0 0 0 1 1	ID = $43
0 0 1 0 n n n n	substatus = 2/n = channel number
0 1 1 1 1 0 1 1	format number = $7B
0 u u u u u u u	u = file name
↓	
0 u u u u u u u	(ASCII - 11 chars.)
1 1 1 1 0 1 1 1	EOX

FORMAT C

1 1 1 1 0 0 0 0	status = $F0
0 1 0 0 0 0 1 1	ID = $43
0 0 1 0 n n n n	substatus = 2 / n = channel number
0 1 1 1 1 1 1 0	format number = $7E
0 a a a a a a a	a = classification name
↓	
0 a a a a a a a	(ASCII - 4 chars.)
0 m m m m m m m	m = data format name
↓	
0 m m m m m m m	(ASCII - 6 chars.)
1 1 1 1 0 1 1 1	EOX

Note 1) FORMAT A type; Request a bulk data of format type f.
FORMAT B type; Request a bulk data with specified file name.
FORMAT C type; Request a bulk data with specified file header.

2) The format of file name is below;

byte 1 - 8 ; file name 8 chars.
byte 9 - 11; extension 3 chars.
total 11 bytes

MESSAGE

SUBSTATUS = 6

FORMAT

1 1 1 1 0 0 0 0	status = $F0
0 1 0 0 0 0 1 1	ID = $43
0 1 1 0 n n n n	substatus = 6/n = channel number
0 x x x x x x x	x = message number
1 1 1 1 0 1 1 1	EOX

TABLE OF MESSAGE

x	message	x	message	x	message	x	message
0	x on	32		64		96	
1	x off	33		65		97	
2	ACK	34		66		98	
3	NAK	35		67		99	
4	Cancel	36		68		100	
5		37		69		101	
6		38		70		102	
7		39		71		103	
8		40		72		104	
9		41		73		105	
10		42		74		106	
11		43		75		107	
12		44		76		108	
13		45		77		109	
14		46		78		110	
15		47		79		111	
16		48		80		112	
17		49		81		113	
18		50		82		114	
19		51		83		115	
20		52		84		116	
21		53		85		117	
22		54		86		118	
23		55		87		119	
24		56		88		120	
25		57		89		121	
26		58		90		122	
27		59		91		123	
28		60		92		124	
29		61		93		125	
30		62		94		126	
31		63		95		127	

INSTRUMENT CLASSIFIED EXCLUSIVE

SUBSTATUS = 7

FORMAT

```
1 1 1 1 0 0 0 0     status = $F0
0 1 0 0 0 0 1 1     ID = $43
0 1 1 1 n n n n     substatus = 7
                    n = instrument classification ID

0 d d d d d d d
       ↓            d = following data
0 d d d d d d d
1 1 1 1 0 1 1 1     EOX
```

TABLE OF CLASSIFICATION ID NUMBER

n	classfication	note
0	ELECTONE	
1	PIANO	includes electronic piano, and with audio accompaniment
2	SYNTHESIZER	combo keyboard (exclude piano)
3	PORTA-INSTRUMENT	Portatone, Portasound etc., multi-functionalized single keyboard
4	P.A. EQUIPMENT	mixer, amplifier, delay, reverb, recorder, etc.
5	COMPUTER	YIS, MSX, etc.
6		
7		
8		
9		
10		
11		
12		
13		
14		
15	EXTENSION	

Note 1) The format of "following data" area is specified by each instrument classification.

Terminology Guide

This expanded index covers MIDI and related synthesis terminology. We have referenced each term to the appropriate book in **The Ferro Music Technology Series**. The page numbers given for MIDI terms in this book reference to formal definitions of terms and/or formats. The page numbers listed for MIDI terms in the other books reference to examples of practical applications. Since most MIDI applications revolve around synthesizers and audio devices, we've also included basic synthesis and audio terms here as well. These terms have been referenced by page numbers to the book, and lesson numbers to the video tape.

The MIDI Book thoroughly covers MIDI applications and interfacing from the end-user's point of view. In it you will find examples of how the messages and concepts defined by the MIDI specification are put to use in the real world. The musical significance of each MIDI message, system designs, and MIDI/non-MIDI synchronization are examples of some of the topics covered in this book.

The Secrets of Analog and Digital Synthesis (listed here as "Secrets") is a complete course in synthesizer sound design. The techniques given in the course are based on musical applications of the physics of sound and can be used with any type of synthesizer. You'll find out how to make use of the synthesizer parameters that can be manipulated with MIDI messages.

Terminology Guide

	Resource Book	MIDI Book	Secrets Book	Secrets Video
Active Sensing	61	44		
Additive Synthesis			98	Lesson 5
After Touch	57	37,66	63, 85	Lesson 3,4
Amplifier			40	Lesson 2
Amplitude			11	Lesson 1
Basic Channel	54	41, 63		
Bit		15		
Block Diagram			72	
Carrier			100	Lesson 5
Channel Message	53,57,59	35,63,65		
Channel Pressure	57	37		
Common Message	53,60	43		
Continuous Controller	57	36,67	63	Lesson 3
Data Bytes	54	34		
Decibel			13	Lesson 1
Drum/Rhythm Machines		86		
Envelope Generator			53	Lesson 3
EOX	62	45		
Exclusive Message	53 ,62	45		
Filter			41	Lesson 2
FM			62	Lesson 3
FM Algorithims			111	Lesson 5
FM Synthesis			100	Lesson 5
Frequency			14	Lesson 1
Harmonic Series			18	Lesson 1
LFO			57	Lesson 3
Local Control	59	38,47		
Message	53	5,54		
MIDI	51	28		
Mode Message	53,59	38,63		
Modulator			100	Lesson 5
Mono	54	39		
Note On/Off	57	36		
Omni On/Off	54	39		
Operator			92	Lesson 5

	Resource Book	MIDI Book	Secrets Book	Secrets Video
Oscillator			33	Lesson 2
Partial			16	Lesson 1
PD Synthesis			86	Lesson 4
Pitch Bender	57	36,66	64,80	Lesson 3, 4
Poly	54	39		
Program Change	57	50		
Real Time Message	53,61	44,74,85		
Ring Modulator			61,84	Lesson 3,4
Running Status	54			
Sample	75			
Sample and Hold			58	Lesson 4
Sample Length	75			
Sample Rate	75			
Sequencer		20,74		
Sideband			61,100	Lesson 5
Song Position Pointer	60	43		
Song Select	60	43		
Spectrum			17	Lesson 1
Start, Stop, Continue	61	44,85		
Status Byte	54	34		
System Messages	53,60,61,62	43		
Timing Clock	61	44,74		
Tune	60	43		
Tuning Ratio			103	Lesson 5
UART	52			
Undefined Status	54			
Unimplemented Status	54			
Velocity	57	48	63,84	Lesson 3,4
Voice		6		
Voice Messages	53,57	35,65		
Waveshape			6	Lesson 1

SECTION 4: REFERENCES AND RESOURCES

In this section:

Lisitings

Lists of music technology resources including:

- MIDI Organizations
- Manufacturers
- On-Line MIDI Resources/Electronic Bulletin Boards
- Educational Sources
- Books and Publications
- Technical Support Facilities

Registration Form

Use this form to register implementation charts, System Exclusive formats, or other data for inclusion in the next edition of **The MIDI Reference Series.**

The MMA: MIDI Manufacturers Association
(as of September 1986)

MMA
2265 Westwood Blvd.
Box 2223
Los Angeles, CA 90064

Adams-Smith
AKG Acoustics
ART
C.T.M
Dynacord
E-mu Systems
Fender Musical Instruments
Forte Music
GPI
Hammond Organ Company
High Technology Dist. Co.
Hybrid Arts
Jellinghaus Musik Systeme
Key Concepts
Laubach Software
Lowrey Industries, Inc.
Microfanatics
Oberheim
Passport Designs, Inc.
Rolandcorp US
SM Elektronik AG
Southworth Music Systems
Syntech
Teac/Tascam
TOA Electronics
Yamaha International Corp.
After Science
Apple Computer
Clarity
Digidesign
Electronic Music Company, Inc.
Ensoniq Corporation
Ferro Technologies
General Electro Music (GEM)
Gulbransen II
Harmony Systems
Matt. Hohner
IDP
J. L. Cooper Electronics
Kurzweil
Lexicon, Inc.
Lync Systems
New England Digital Corp.
Octave-Plateau Electronics
PPG
Sequential
Sound Creation LTD
SSL Limited
Synthaxe
Telex Communications
Unicord/Korg

Japanese MIDI Standards Commitee
(partial listing)

JMSC
Gakki Kaikan
2-18-21 Sotokan
Chiyoda-Ku
Tokyo, 101
Japan

Akai
Kawai
Roland
Casio
Korg
Yamaha

International MIDI Association

IMA
11857 Hartsook Street
North Hollywood
CA 91607

"The International MIDI Association is dedicated to the accurate dissemination of information pertaining to the Musical Instrument Digital Interface (MIDI). "

There are three classes of IMA membership:

Hardware/Software Manufacturer, Manufacturer/Developer
Retailer/Educator
End-User Technician

Contact the IMA for membership details.

360 Systems
18730 Oxnard Street
#215
Tarzana, CA 91356

Adams - Smith
34 Tower Street
Hudson, MA 01749

Akai
Box 2344
Fort Worth, TX 76113

AKG Acoustics
2 Calvin Road
Watertown, MA 02172

Apple Computer
20525 Mariani Drive
Cupertino, CA 95124

ART
215 Tremont Street
Rochester, NY 14608

Atari
Box 61657
Sunnyvale, CA 94088

Bacchus Software
2210 Wilshire Blvd
Suite 330
Santa Monica, CA 90430

Beam Team
6100 Adeline
Oakland, CA 94608

Blank Software
1034 Natoma Street
San Francisco, CA 94103

Caged Artist Productions
64 Griggs Street
Brookline, MA 02146

Casio
15 Gardner Road
Fairfield, NJ 07006

Clarity
Nelson Lane
Garrison, NY 10524

Club MIDI Software
P.O. Box 93895
Hollywood, CA 91605

Commodore International
1200 Wilson
Westchester, PA 19380

CTM Development
Case Postale 82
CH-1213 Petit Lancey
2 Switzerland

Decillonix
P.O. Box 70895
Sunnyvale, CA 94086

Digidesign
920 Commercial Street
Palo Alto, CA 94303

Dr. T's Music Software
66 Louise Road
Chestnut Hill, MA 02167

E-mu Systems
1600 Green Hills Road
Scotts Valley, CA 95066-0303

Electronic Arts
2755 Campus Drive
San Mateo, CA 94403

Ensoniq Corporation
263 Great Valley Parkway
Malvern, PA 19355

Fairlight Instruments (US)
2945 Westwood Blvd.
Los Angeles, CA 90064

Fender Musical Instruments
1300 Valencia Drive
Fullerton, CA 92631

Ferro Technologies
228 Washington Ave
Belleville, NJ 07109

Forat Electronics
11514 Ventura Blvd
Unit 1 &2
Studio City, CA 91604

Forte Music
P.O. Box 6322
San Jose, CA 95150

Fostex Corp.
15431 Blackburn Ave
Norwalk, CA 90650

Friend-Chip
Bergmanstrasse
1000 Berlin 64
West Germany

Garfield Electronics
Box 1941
Burbank, CA 91507

General Electro Music (GEM)
1260 Mark Street
Oak Grove Village, IL 60007

Great Wave Software
104 Gilbert Ave
Menlo Park, CA 94025

Gulbransen II
3132 Jefferson Street
San Diego, CA 92110

Hammond Organ Company
4200 Diversey Avenue
Chicago, IL 60639

Harmony Systems
4405 International
B-113
Norcross, GA 30093

Hinton Instruments
168 Abingdon Road
Oxford, OX1 4RA
England

Hybrid Arts, Inc.
11720 W. Olympic Blvd.
Los Angeles, CA 90064

IDP
1109 Parklane
Suite 200
Witchita, KS 67210

Indus Systems
9304 Deering Ave
Chatsworth, CA 91311

J. L. Cooper Electronics
1931 Pontius Avenue
West Los Angeles, CA 90025

Jellinghaus Musik Systeme
Friedof 6-8
46 Dortmund
West Germany

Kanlet Electronics
Box 916
Indian Hills, CA 80454

KAT
43 Meadow Road
Longmeadow, MA 01106

Key Clique
3960 Laurel Canyon
Studio City, CA 91604

Korg USA
89 Frost Street
Westbury, NY 11590

Kurzweil
411 Waverley Oaks Road
Waltham, MA 02154

Lexicon, Inc.
60 Turner Street
Waltham, MA 02154

Lowrey Industries, Inc.
825 E. 26th Street
La Grange Park, IL 60525

Lync Systems, Inc.
P.O. Box
1416 Schenectady, NY 12301

Magnetic Music
P.O. Box 328
Rhinebeck, NY 12572

Mark Of The Unicorn
222 Third Street
Cambridge, MA 02142

Midimix
Box 161
Ashland, OR 97520

Mimetics
P.O. Box 60238
Station A
Palo Alto, CA 94306

Moog Electronics
2500 Walden Ave
Buffalo, NY 14225

Musicsoft
P.O. Box 274
Beekman, NY 12750

Musicworks
18 Haviland Street
Boston, MA 02115

New England Digital Corp.
P.O. Box 546
White River Junction, VT 05047

Oberheim
11650 W. Olympic Blvd.
Los Angeles, CA 90064

Octave-Plateau Electronics
51 Main Street
Yonkers, NY 10701

Opcode Systems
1040 Ramona
Palo Alto, CA 94301

Panasonic
One Panasonic Way
Secaucus, NJ 07094

Passport Designs, Inc.
625 Miramontes Street
Half Moon Bay, CA 94019

PPG
Wandsbeker Vollstrasse
87-89/N3 D-2000
Hamburg, West Germany

Rolandcorp US
7200 Dominion Circle
Los Angeles, CA 90040-3647

Sequential
3051 North First Street
San Jose, CA 95134

Siel
(c/o On-Site Music)
3000 Marcus Ave
Lake Success, NY 11042

Sonus
24130 Strathern
Suite H
Canoga Park, CA 91304

Southworth Music Sytems
91 Ann Lee Road
Harvard, MA 01451

SSL Limited
Stonesfield, Oxford
OX7 2PQ, England

Standard Productions
1314 34th Ave.
San Francisco, CA 94122

Synchronous Technologies
Box 14467
102 W. Wilshire Blvd
Oklahoma City, OK 73113

Syntech
23958 Craftsman Road
Calabasas, CA 91032

Synthaxe Limited
Four Season House
102B Woodstock Road
Witney, Oxfordshire OX8 6DY UK

Teac/Tascam
7733 Telegraph Road
Montebello, CA 90640

Valhala Music, Inc.
Box 20157
Ferndale, MI 48220

Voyce Music
13476 Calle Colina
Poway, CA 92064

Voyetra Technologies
426 Mount Pleasant Ave.
Mamaroneck, NY 10543

Yamaha International Corp.
6600 Orangethorpe Ave.
Buena Park, CA 90620

Zaphod Electronics
220 Diablo Ave
Mountain View, CA 94043

American MIDI Users Group
7225 Fair Oaks, Suite 515
Dallas, Texas 75231
Voice: 214 272-0963
Voice: 214 987-2940
Data : 214 276-8902

Music Terminal
Data #1: 714 545-5768
Data #2: 714 524-9326

ESI/IMC SYNTHNET
183 North Martel Ave.
Suite 205
Los Angeles , CA 90036
Voice: 213 937-0347

254 W 54th ST.
Penthouse
New York, NY 10019
212 757-0320

Canadian West Coast
MIDI Users Group
4538 Marquerite Street
Vancouver, B.C. Canada
V6J4G8
Data: 604 263-8487

KCB Systems
Computer Music BBS
P.O. Box 1733
Denton, Texas 76202
Voice: 817 565-0730
Data: 817 382-5778

Mirco Music MIDI BBS
210 Marry Dr.
Alanta, GA. 30341
Data: 404 454-8059
Voice: 1-800 551-4251

MIDI-COM (Montreal)
483 Neptune
Dorval, Quebec CANADA
H9S 2L7
Data: 514-744-7354

The Mixing Board
Data: 718-479-9874

MIDI Manufacturers Assn. BBS
C/O Jim Cooper J.L. Cooper Electronics
1931 Pontius Avenue
West Los Angeles, CA 90025
Voice: 213-473-8771

Canadian MIDI Users Group BBS
P.O. Box 1043
Belleville, Ontario
Canada
K8N 5B6

COMPUSERVE MIDI/Musicforums
P.O. Box 20212
Columbus, Ohio 43220
617 457-6650

Hybrid Arts
213 826-4288

MIDI Connection
212 594-2646

Alphasyntauri Users Group BBS
Data: 201 661-1249

MIDI Conference Area
LFD Enterprises BBS
Data: 317-875-7773

MIDI WORLD NETWORK
11920 W. Olympic Blvd.
L.A., CA 90064
Voice: 213-826-3777
Data: 213-826-4288

Musician's Exchange
Data: 619-462-5229

MusicNet
P.O. Box 272
Beekman, N.Y. 12570
Data: 914-442-4006
Data: 1-800-643-7968
Voice: 914-724-3668

GEnie
Voice: 800-638-8369

SNAPP MIDI Board
Data: 714-921-2255

Synergy BBS
Voice: 415-961-3811

Performing Artists Network (PAN)
P.O. Box 162
Skippack, PA 19474
Data: 215-489-4640
Voice: 1-800-544-4005

SuperService East
2102 Osceola SE
Grand Rapids, MI 49606
Voice: 616-245-6635

Mid West MIDI BBS
3408 Meadowbrook Dr.
Mid West City, Oklahoma 73110
Data & Voice: 405-733-3102

MIDI LINE
DATA: 613-966-6823

University of Arizona School Of Music
Tuscon
AZ 85721

California Polytechnic State University
Music Dept.
San Luis Obispo
CA 93407

California State University, Los Angeles
Music Dept. 5151 State University Drive
Los Angeles
CA 90032

Fullerton College
Music Dept. 321 E. Chapman Ave.
Fullerton
CA 92634

Dick Grove School Of Music
12754 Ventura Blvd.
Studio City
CA 91604

Los Angeles Recording Workshop
5287 Sunset Blvd.
Hollywood
CA 90027

Los Medanos College
2700 E. Leland Rd.
Pittsburgh
CA 94565

Sonoma State University
1801 E. Cotati Ave.
Rohnert Park
CA 94928

University Of California, San Diego
La Jolla
CA 92093

University Of Chicago
Office Of Continuing Education, 5835 S.Kimbark Ave.
Chicago
IL 60637

Ball State University
School Of Music
Muncie
IN 47306

Kansas State University
Music Dept.
Manhattan
KS 66506

Berklee College Of Music
1140 Boylston St.
Boston
MA 02215

BEEP Studios
33 Elm Street
Brookline, MA 02147

Harvard University
Electronic Music Studio
Cambridge, MA 02138

New England Conservatory
Electronic Music Studio
290 Huntington Ave.
Boston, MA 02115

New Jersey Institute Of Technology
Dr. Martin Luther King Blvd.
Newark
NJ 07102

Montclair State College
Music Dept, Normal Avenue and Valley Road
Upper Montclair
NJ 07043

Kean State College
Music Dept., Morris Avenue
Union
NJ 07083

New Mexico State University
Music Dept. Box 3F
Los Croces
NM 88003

Center For The Media Arts
Conservatory of Music For The Media
226 W. 26th St,
New York
NY 10001

Institute Of Audio Research
64 University Place, Greenwich Village
New York
NY 10003

Musication
1206 Bay Ridge Ave.
Brooklyn
NY 11216

P.A.S.S. (Public Access Synthesizer Studio)
16 West 22nd St. (902)
New York
NY 10010

University Of North Carolina At Asheville
Music Dept. One University Heights
Asheville
NC 28804

The Recording Workshop
455 Massieville Rd.
Chillicothe
OH 45601

Lincoln Institute
7622 Louetta Rd.
Spring
TX 77379

New England Digital
Seminar, Box 546
White River Jct
VT 05001

BOOKS

Secrets Of Analog and Digital Synthesis
Steve De Furia
Third Earth Productions
Hal Leonard Books

The MIDI BOOK: Using MIDI and Related Interfaces
Steve De Furia, Joe Scacciaferro
Third Earth Productions
Hal Leonard Books

The MIDI Implementation Book
Steve De Furia, Joe Scacciaferro
Third Earth Productions
Hal Leonard Books

The MIDI System Exclusive Book
Steve De Furia, Joe Scacciaferro
Third Earth Productions
Hal Leonard Books

The MIDI Resource Book
Steve De Furia, Joe Scacciaferro
Third Earth Productions
Hal Leonard Books

The Complete DX7
Howard Massey
Amsco Publications
Dist. Music Sales

Yamaha DX7 Digital Synthesizer
Yasuhiko Fukada
Amsco Publications
Rittor Music

MIDI For Musicians
Craig Anderton
Amsco Publications
Music Sales

MIDI 1.0 Detailed Specification
MMA/JMSC Document
Available through the IMA

Start Me Up: The Music Biz Meets the Personal Computer
Benjamin Krepack, Rod Firestone

The Art Of Electronic Music
(collected from Keyboard magazine)
GPI Books

MIDI • Programming • Software
(collected from Keyboard magazine)
GPI Books

Beginning Synthesizer
GPI Books

Synthesizer Technique
(collected from Keyboard magazine)
GPI Books

Synthesizers and Computers
(collected from Keyboard magazine)
GPI Books

The Whole Synthesizer Catalog
(collected from Keyboard magazine)
GPI Books

Instructional Video

The Secrets Of Analog and Digital Synthesis: Video Tape
Ferro Productions
DCI Music Videos

Periodicals

One-Two Testing
First Floor, Berkshire House
168-173 High Holborn
London, WC1V 7AU
England

Computer Music Journal
MIT Press
28 Carleton Street
Cambridge, MA 02142

Modern Drummer
870 Pompton Avenue
Cedar Grove, N J 07009

Modern Percussionist
870 Pompton Avenue
Cedar Grove, N J 07009

Musician
Box 701
31 Commercial Street
Gloucester, MA 01930

Journal Of The Audio Engineering Association
AES
60 East 42nd Street
New York, NY 10165-0075

Electronic Musician
2608 Ninth Street
Berkeley, CA 94710

Mix Magazine
2608 Ninth Street
Berkeley, CA 94710

Keyboard
20085 Stevens Creek Blvd.
Cupertino, CA 95014

Guitar Player
20085 Stevens Creek Blvd.
Cupertino, CA 95014

Roland User's Group
7200 Dominion Circle
Los Angeles, CA 90040

The IMA Bulletin
11857 Hartsook Street
North Hollywood, CA 91607

After Touch
Box 2338
Northridge, CA 91323

Technical Support Facilities

The following is a list of technical support facilities throughout the USA. The list was derived from polling service managers from several of the industry's leading manufacturers, and also from the recommendations of musicians in the areas local to the facilities. Our final selections were based on multiple recommendations.

All of these facilities provide the expertise necessary to support maintenance, operation, and custom design (modifications) of today's most sophisticated equipment.

This list is not to be perceived as complete or final. We will continue to update it in future editions. (See the **Registration Form** at the end of this section.) Take the time to research the service facilities in your area (use this list as a starting point); they can be one of your greatest allies in your efforts to perform with today's technology.

Synthony Music
4228 Craftsman Ct.
Scottsdale, AZ 85251
(602) 945-0368

Advanced Musical Electronics
3762 Overland Ave.
W. Los Angeles, CA 90034
(213) 478-0589

CAE Sound
1150 E. Santa Inez
San Mateo, CA 94401

High Tech
2800 South Washington Blvd.
Marina Del Rey, CA 90292
(213) 822-1893

Linear Sound
5427 Telegraph Ave.
Oakland, CA 94609

Paul Morte Technical Services
635-K N. Eckhoff
Orange, CA 92668
(714) 634-2371

Music Tech
11914 Ventura Blvd.
Studio City, CA 91604
(818) 506-4055

Skips Music
2740 Auburn Blvd.
Sacramento, CA 95821
(916) 484-7575

Ace Music
13630 W. Dixies Hwy.
N. Miami, FL 33161
(305) 891-6281

Thoroughbred
2202 E. Hillsboro Ave.
Tampa, FL 33612
(813) 238-6485

Specialized Audio
490 Armour Circle NE
Atlanta, GA 30324

Wizard Electronics
1438-40 Tullie Circle
Atlanta, GA 30329
(404) 325-4891

Carmalou's Music
4110 Center Point Rd. N.E.
Cedar Rapids, IA
(319) 393-3121

Advanced Technical Service
3725 N. 25th
Schiller Park, IL 60176
(312) 678-8828

Excelandt Servicing, Inc.
666 E. Northwest Highway
Mt. Prospect, IL 60056
(312) 259-2829

Spectrum Sound
3533 W. 30th St.
Indianapolis, IN 46222
(317) 923-7868

Miller Music
445 N. West St.
Witchita, KS 67203
(316) 942-7341

Syntronics
475 Commonwealth Ave.
Boston, MA 02115
(617) 266-5039

Arnold Williams Music
& Sound Solution
5702 Canton Center Rd.
Canton, MI 48187
(313) 453-6586

EMI
2852 Johnson Street NE
Minn. MN 55418
(612) 789-2496

Good Guys
1111 Grand Ave.
St. Paul, MN 55105
(612) 292-9165

Triple S Electronics
228 Washington Ave.
Belleville, NJ 07109
(201) 751-0481

D.B. Musical Electronics
632 Walden Ave.
Buffalo., NY 14211
(716) 894-9426

Triple S Electronics
240 W. 55th
New York, NY 10019
(201) 751-0481

Computer Music Systems
1626 Glennwood Ave.
Reynolds, NC 27608
(919) 833-9432

PI Keyboards
2121 Brookpark Road
Cleveland, OH 44134
(216) 741-1400

Secret Service
4112 Gordon St.
Cincinnati, OH 45223
(513) 451-2292

K.M.A Electronics
1733 SE. Morrison
Portland, OR 97214
(903) 503-6552

Bentons Elec. Service
1514 Ahrens
Houston, TX 77017
(713) 641-4944

Lightning Music
4801 Spring Valley #103A
Dallas, TX 75244
(214)387-1198

Strait Music
908 N. Lamar
Autin, TX 78703
(512) 476-6927

Carlo Sound
2 Music Circle E.
Nashville, TN 37203
(615) 259-0900

Uncle Bobs
6653 West Capitol Drive
Milwaukee , WI 53216
(414) 462-2700

Registration For Future Editions

All three books in the **MIDI Reference Series** will be updated periodically to keep pace with the evolution of MIDI. If you would like your company and/or products to be represented in the appropriate sections of future editions of **The MIDI Resource Book, The MIDI Implementation Book,** or **The MIDI System Exclusive Book**, please send the documentation (printed material or MacWrite compatible diskettes) along with a completed copy of the registration form below to:

Ferro Technologies
Dept. 13
228 Washington Avenue
Belleville, NJ 07109

Registration Form

COMPANY: ______________________

ADDRESS: ______________________

CITY: ______________________

STATE | PROVINCE: ______________________

COUNTRY: ______________________

PHONE | TELEX: ______________________

CONTACT: ______________________

AFFILIATION: JMSC ☐ MMA ☐ IMA ☐ OTHER ☐ NONE ☐

LISTING TYPE:

☐ IMP CHART LISTING
☐ SYSEX LISTING
☐ MANUFACTURER LISTING
☐ MIDI ORGANIZATION LISTING
☐ BBS LISTING
☐ BOOK & PUBLICATION LISTING
☐ SERVICE CENTER LISTING
☐ EDUCTATION LISTING